Phonics in Proper Perspective

Arthur W. Heilman
The Pennsylvania State University

Charles E. Merrill Publishing Company
Columbus, Ohio
A Bell and Howell Company

Library of Congress Catalog Card Number: 68-8825

PRINTED IN THE UNITED STATES
OF AMERICA

1   2   3   4   5   6 — 73   72   71   70   69   68

Preface

The second edition of this book starts from the same premise as the first edition: children *must* learn to associate printed letters with the speech sounds they represent. This skill is so important that it should be taught systematically and taught well.

Another premise is that the good reader uses phonic skills, context clues, and sight vocabulary in combination because *these skills work together*. The beginning reader must grasp this fact, and to help him do so instruction should emphasize these skills concomitantly, not sequentially.

While adults may never have agreed on an answer to the question, "What is Reading?", all children develop a *set* as to what it is. Beginning instruction determines this set. Once we have instilled in a young child that reading is either "sounding all words" or learning all "words-as-wholes," it is often most difficult to teach him to extinguish these responses. The history of reading instruction in America is a chronicle of frustration which stems in part from our predilection to make beginning reading consist *exclusively* of letter sound analysis— or from ignoring this skill for a period of time.

It would not be a tragedy if adults continued their fruitless *either-or* debate except for the fact that one side or the other is always dominant. Teaching materials swing with the winner and many children's reading ability suffers as a result. Good instruction will avoid teaching a child to overrely on one skill. Facile reading is built on a balanced mastery of sight words, letter-sound analysis, and the use of context clues.

A third premise of the book is that teachers should understand the educational issues which underlie the various alternative approaches to cracking the code. Therefore, a number of newer approaches to teaching beginning reading are discussed from the standpoint of how they approach this problem. The objective of Chapter 5 is not to provide a blueprint for the use of i.t.a., linguistic materials, *Words in Color*, programmed reading, and diacritical marking systems; rather, it is to point up the underlying strategies these materials employ to arrive at the same goal.

Another purpose of the book is to provide both the experienced and the prospective teacher with materials which might lead to a better understanding of:

1. the purpose and limitations of phonics instruction as it relates to teaching reading;
2. concrete practices which may be followed in teaching the various "steps" in phonic analysis; and
3. the rationale which underlies particular instructional practices.

As teachers, we need to be well informed about both what to teach and why we teach as we do. Otherwise, methodology may become separated from logical principles of learning. In recent years this has actually happened in much of the discussion of phonics as well as in practices advocated by certain critics of present-day reading instruction.

I would like to thank Mrs. Jane Johnson and Miss Julie Estadt of the Merrill Production Staff for their assistance throughout the publication of this book.

Table of Contents

1   The Purpose and Limitations of Phonics Instruction, 1

Word Analysis Skills, 4
Skills in Combination, 6
Essential Concomitant Learnings, 11
Teaching Rules for Sounding, 15
Principles to Apply in Teaching Phonics, 21
Steps in Teaching Phonics, 23

2   Teaching Auditory-Visual Discrimination and Association of Consonant Letter-Sounds, 26

Phonics Instruction Related to Previous Learnings, 26
Teaching Auditory Discrimination, 27
Teaching Visual Discrimination, 30
Teaching Consonant Sounds, 31
Teaching Contractions, 46
Summary of Consonant Generalizations, 47
Summary, 48

3   Teaching Vowel Sounds, 53

Teaching Short *A* Sound, 54
Short Sound of *I*, 56
Teaching the Short Sound of *E*, 58
Short Sound of *U*, 58
Short Sound of *O*, 59
Teaching Short Sound of Initial and Medial Vowels as One Generalization, 60
The Schwa Sound, 61
Teaching Long and Short Sounds Together, 66

Examples of Exercises for Teaching Vowel Sounds, **67**
Exceptions to Vowel Rules Previously Taught, **67**
Vowel Sounds Affected by *R*, **68**
The OO Sounds, **69**
Diphthongs, **70**
Homonyms, **72**
Summary, **72**
Sight-Word List and Informal Phonics Test, **73**

4   Syllabication: Prefixes, Suffixes, and Accent, 77

Syllabication, **77**
Rules for Breaking Words into Syllables, **78**
Teaching Prefixes and Suffixes as Units, **81**
Forming Plurals, **84**
Compound Words, **85**
Finding Little Words in Big Words, **88**
Accent, **88**
Stress on Words Within Sentences, **90**
Use of the Dictionary—As a Word Attack Skill, **91**
Conclusion, **91**

5   Alternative Approaches to Cracking the Code, 93

Criticism Leads to New Materials, **95**
Linguistic (Regular Spelling) Approach, **95**
Teaching Based on Regular Spellings, **100**
Overlearning Certain Visual-Sound Patterns, **101**
Code Cracking with a Missing Ingredient, **102**
Initial Teaching Alphabet (i.t.a.), **103**
Words in Color, **108**
Programmed Reading, **110**
Diacritical Marking System, **111**
Conclusion, **112**

BIBLIOGRAPHY, 116

INDEX, 119

Chapter 1

The Purpose and Limitations of Phonics Instruction

The purpose of phonics instruction, as it relates to reading, is to provide the reader with the ability to associate printed letters with the speech sounds that these letters represent. In *applying* phonic skills to an unknown word the reader blends a series of sounds dictated by the order in which particular letters occur in the printed word. One needs this ability in order to arrive at the pronunciation of printed word symbols which are not instantly recognized. Obviously, if one recognizes a printed word he should not puzzle over the speech sounds represented by the individual letters.

It should not be implied that "arriving at the pronunciation" of a word means that the child is learning *how* to pronounce that word. In most reading situations, particularly in the primary grades, the reader knows the pronunciation of practically all of the words he will meet in his reading. What he does not know is that the printed word symbol *represents* the pronunciation of a particular word that he uses and understands in his oral language. Through phonic analysis he resolves this dilemma.

Phonics does not constitute a method for teaching the complicated process called reading. To keep the teaching of phonics in proper perspective, one must: (1) see phonic analysis as an absolutely essential reading skill; (2) realize that phonics is one of a number of ways a child may "solve" words not known as sight words; (3) understand that learning to overrely on phonics, sight words, or context clues can produce serious reading problems.

1

In recent years, noticeable confusion has accompanied discussions of reading because the meanings of some of the terms used in those discussions were vague or misleading. Certain critics of reading instruction tried to establish the existence of a dichotomy in which reading instruction was attempted by means of teaching exclusively either sight words or phonics. Linguists have rightly pointed out that the terms phonics and phonetics are often used interchangeably despite the fact that these terms have quite different meanings. In an effort to militate against further confusion, a few brief definitions of basic terms are presented here:

1. *Phonics instruction* — A facet of reading instruction which (1) leads the child to understand that printed letters in printed words represent the speech sounds heard when words are pronounced; (2) involves the actual teaching of which sound is associated with a particular letter or combination of letters.

2. *Phonic analysis* — The process of *applying* knowledge of letter-sound relationships, i.e., blending the sounds represented by letters so as to arrive at the pronunciation of printed words.

3. *Phonetics* — That segment of linguistic science which deals with speech sounds, how these sounds are made vocally, sound changes which develop in languages, and the relation of speech sounds to the total language process. All phonics instruction is derived from phonetics, but phonics (as it relates to reading) utilizes only a relatively small portion of the body of knowledge identified as phonetics.

4. *Word analysis* — An inclusive term which categorizes methods of recognizing words which are not known as sight words. (Discussed in detail later in this chapter.)

5. *Sight-word method* — The term "sight-word method" is an abstraction which does not adequately describe present-day reading instruction. However, most beginning reading materials developed in the past thirty years involved the teaching of a limited number of sight words before phonic analysis was introduced. The term "sight-word method" came into common usage even though it actually described only this initial teaching procedure. Gradually the term was used to imply the existence of an instructional approach which proscribed phonics and advocated teaching every new word by sight only.

6. *Phonetic method* — Since there is no exclusive phonic method of teaching reading, this term sometimes functions as either an abstraction or overstatement. For example, if "phonetic method" simply means that phonic analysis is employed, all methods of teaching reading would qualify as phonetic methods. On the other hand, if phonetic method implies teaching reading by means of exclusive reliance on phonic analysis, all presently acceptable definitions of reading would have to be discarded. "Word analysis" could be substituted for read-

ing and children could be punished each time a word was learned as a sight word. Also, English word spellings would have to be completely revised along phonetic principles. This change has been suggested by some groups; but while the idea has certain merits, no wholesale revision has as yet been accepted.

7. *Phonetic method vs. sight-word method* — These terms have often been used to suggest the existence of two antithetical approaches to teaching reading. In reality, no such dichotomy exists and teachers of reading should not use such terms in this sense. Nor should critics who use them in this sense go unchallenged.

8. *Alphabetic principle* — Graphic symbols have been devised for representing a large number of spoken languages. Three types of writing (picture, ideographic, and alphabetic), indicated below, represent the English words or concepts *car, carp* (a fish), *carpet.*

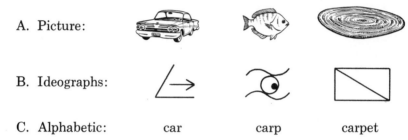

A. Picture:

B. Ideographs:

C. Alphabetic: car   carp   carpet

Examples A and B are purely arbitrary. The ideographs in B are not taken from an established language. The most important feature of the ideographic writing is that there are no common features in the three symbols. Example C is also arbitrary, but the symbols and their *order of occurrence* have been universally agreed upon since they are taken from English writing. The first three letter-symbols in each word are identical. They signal the reader to blend the same three speech sounds (phonemes) if his goal is to arrive at the spoken word that the various letter configurations represent.

There are many other spoken words in which one hears the same three phonemes in the same sequence. The graphic representation of these speech sounds will be the same in each printed word: *carnival, cardinal, card, cartoon.* However, in English writing one may *see* the graphic symbols *car* and find they represent different phonemes than the ones under discussion (carol, care, career, caress, caret).

9. *Phoneme* — The smallest unit of sound in a language. Pronouncing the word *cat* involves the blending of three phonemes, /k/ /æ/ /t/.

10. *Grapheme* — A written or printed letter-symbol used to *represent* a speech sound or phoneme.

11. *Grapheme-phoneme relationship* — This term refers to the relationship between printed letters and the sounds they represent, and

would also cover the deviations found in such a relationship. Thus, while English writing is based on an alphabetic code, there is not a one-to-one relationship between graphemes (printed symbols) and phonemes (speech sounds) they represent. Some printed symbols represent several different sounds (*car*, *caress*, *cake*); and one speech sound may be represented by a large number of different letters or combinations of letters (discussed later in this chapter). To a large extent, this problem stems from the spelling patterns of words which have become established in English writing.

12. Morphemes — The smallest meaningful units of language. The word *cat* is a morpheme whose pronunciation consists of three phonemes. If one wishes to speak of more than one cat the letter *s* forming the plural cat*s* becomes a morpheme since it changes the meaning as does the possessive *'s* in *the cat's dinner*.

There are two classes of morphemes, *free* and *bound*. The former functions independently in any utterance (house, lock, man, want). Bound morphemes must combine with other morphemes, such as prefixes, suffixes, and inflectional endings (house*s*, *un*lock, man*'s*, want*ed*).

13. *Cracking the code*—The process of learning to associate printed letters with the speech sounds they represent. Thus, phonics instruction aims to help the child crack the code. Chapter 5 discusses other approaches to cracking the code, most of which include phonics.

Before a child begins to read he has made tremendous progress in mastering his native language. Since linguists define language as "oral or spoken," then print or writing is a "graphic representation" of language. Alphabets are codes. Learning to read involves learning the relationship between printed symbols and spoken words. As one progresses in mastering the relationship between print and spoken language, he is cracking the code. When he has learned to associate all of the specific printed letters with specific speech sounds he has mastered or cracked the code. He can now arrive at or approximate the pronunciation of most printed word-symbols. In summary, one must "crack the code" in order to gain independence in reading.

WORD ANALYSIS SKILLS

There are a number of methods that a child might use to determine what spoken word is represented by an unknown printed word. These various approaches for solving unknown words are referred to as *word analysis skills*, which include the following:

1. *Word form* — In general, all words (except homographs: wind-wind, etc.) can be said to be unique in appearance. Yet, in the

experience of a primary-level child, the visual forms of words are so much alike that much practice is needed to perceive the minute differences between them. While learning to discriminate word forms, the child might note such limited factors as the length of words, or special features such as *tt, ll, oo,* or final *y.* Learning to recognize the word *monkey* because it has a tail (y) at the end may serve an immediate and limited purpose; but soon the child will meet money, merry, funny, and penny. The word *look* may be learned as having two eyes in the middle; but soon the child meets book, stood, flood. It is obvious that, as the child expands his reading, these unique features are found in a large number of words and thus become of less and less value.

2. *Structural analysis* — Here, the child may note structural changes which differentiate between words having common roots. Such changes include:

a) the addition of inflectional endings (-s, -ed, -ing)
b) modifications resulting when prefixes or suffixes have been added to known roots (pre-, un-, dis-; -tion, -ment)
c) combining two words to form compounds (anyone, someplace, sidewalk).

3. *Context clues* — When a child is reading for meaning, the context in which an unknown word is met is useful in suggesting what the word might be. Usually, only a few words could possibly fill out the meaning. For example:

"The boy threw the ball to his _____."

Probably less than a dozen words could logically be inserted in the blank space (friend, dog, mother, playmate, sister, father, brother). Some possibilities would be less logical than others depending on what has happened in the story prior to this sentence.

A number of devices are utilized by authors to provide context clues which help readers solve new words and difficult concepts. One of these is to incorporate a description-definition in the text.

"They were now traveling through _____ country. It was very hot, there was sand under foot and the wind blew sand in their eyes. There were no streams — no water whatsoever — and no shade trees. The d_____ extended as far as the eye could see."

Other techniques include comparison or contrast, and the use of synonyms or antonyms.

"At this point the stream flowed very _____ [rapidly]. The water splashed over the rocks and sent up white spray as it moved swiftly through the pass."

Solving the pronunciation of an unknown word is facilitated by:

a) the meaning of the total sentence in which the word occurs
b) what has occurred in previously read sentences and sentences which follow — assuming, of course, that the child is "reading for meaning."

4. *Picture clues* — Certain critics oppose the use of pictures in early reading materials on the ground that some children will over-rely on pictures. If this occurs it interferes with learning to read. Those critical of using pictures often advocate approaches which emphasize code cracking in beginning reading. Usually materials of this nature do not lend themselves to very meaningful illustrations.

It is true that pictures may provide clues to unknown words (turkey, cliff, wagon, father, bridge, fireplace). Pictures may suggest words. In addition, they also have high motivational value and will often lure a young reader into reading. Pictures help focus attention on meaning; they lead into a story, and where only a limited number of words are known, pictures supplement. They serve as stimuli for oral language usage in group discussions.

When children are observed to overrely on picture clues, this fact should have diagnostic significance for the teacher. It suggests that certain instructional practices may need closer examination, rather than that pictures should be proscribed in children's reading materials.

5. *Phonic analysis* — The English alphabet contains twenty-six letters which represent more than forty speech sounds. The difficulty of learning to read English is compounded by the fact that many letters and letter combinations represent a number of different sounds. Despite this lack of consistency in written English, a person learning to read must associate printed letter-symbols with characteristic speech sounds. The teaching of letter-sounds is referred to as "phonics instruction." The various steps in teaching phonics are listed at the end of this chapter and discussed in detail in later chapters.

SKILLS IN COMBINATION

The above approaches to word analysis are probably not of equal value in learning to read. Different children may learn to rely on one method more than on others; and some approaches, such as unique word form, have limited utility beyond the early stages of learning to read. Facile reading would not result if one went through a series of trial-and-error responses in which only one of the above approaches to word analysis was used. Efficient readers use various methods of word attack simultaneously.

Seeing phonics in proper perspective involves: (1) understanding that phonic analysis is one means by which children can "solve" words not known as sight words; (2) noting that phonics relates to, and interacts with, all of the other methods of word analysis. For example, structural and phonic analysis constantly interact. Such prefabricated units as *ex-*, *pre-*, *dis-*, *en-*, *pro-*, *-ed*, *-ing*, *-tive*, *-ment*, *-tion*, and the like, when added to words, do produce structural changes. Each of these, and many more, are also phonic units. The pronunciation of prefixes, suffixes, and compound words remains quite consistent.

Structural changes in a word will often camouflage clues which the reader may have used in recognizing the root. When a child does not instantly recognize such a new word, he should resort to sounding. For example, a child may know the word *locate*, but not recognize *dislocated*, or *relocating*. Sounding the "parts" will unlock the pronunciation and, since the meaning of the root word is known, the meaning of the new word is grasped. A child should not be taught to rely exclusively on one method or approach for solving unknown words. In the incomplete sentence under *context clues*, it was noted that the context permitted several logical choices.

"The boy threw the ball to his _____."

Here the reader was restricted to context alone. But with good instruction he will learn not to rely exclusively on context clues. In addition, in an actual reading situation he would not be confronted with a blank space, but rather a series of letters. Notice that when the reader heeds the initial letter and solves the sound it represents, the number of logical choices is drastically reduced:

"The boy threw the ball to his s - - - - -."

It is doubtful a reader will need more than the minimal clue provided in the first example above. But if he needs to, he may sound and blend more of the letters — *sis* - - -.

Context clues are not limited to the sentence in which the unknown word occurs. For example, assume a child is reading the following sentence in which the blank represents an unknown word:

A. "Look, look," said Jack, "look at the _____."

The content of example A alone does not provide enough context clues for the reader to solve the unknown word. In B, the sentence is shown in a larger context.

B. "I hear a car," said Jack.
"I do not hear a car," said Suzy. "I hear a funny noise."
"I hear a honk-honk," said Jack, "but I do not see a car."
"That noise is in the sky," said Suzy.
Jack pointed at the sky. "Look," said Jack. "Look at the
g - - - -."
Suzy said, "They are flying south for the winter."

At this point, the background and previous experience of some readers will suggest the unknown word. The context suggests several classes of subjects, such as birds or airplanes, which would be logical. However, in the child's book, the unknown is not a blank space, it is a word composed of letters. The sounds which these letters represent have been studied. Even though the word is not known, the child who has been properly taught will note the initial consonant *g*. He will not say *bird* or *airplane* or any other word which does not begin with the *g* sound. He will "sound" as much as he needs:

> "Look at the g - - - -.
> gee - -.
> geese."

This story, since it is at the primary level, is accompanied by a picture which shows both children looking up, with Jack pointing toward the sky to a V formation of geese. Thus, context, previous experience, a picture, sounding the initial consonant, then the double vowel, if needed, all provide clues which will help the reader solve the unknown word without a noticeable hesitation. The less facile reader might require a pause in his reading while he "sounds out" the word. Only a very inefficient reader would have to depend entirely on "sounding" out every letter in the unknown word. This would involve wasting all of the other clues.

Educational Issues in Phonics Instruction

Despite the extended debate on phonics instruction and the general agreement that children *must* learn letter-sound relationships in order to become independent readers, there are still a number of issues that must be dealt with when one begins phonics instruction.

One of these is whether beginning reading instruction should emphasize that reading is a meaning-making process. Second, does the emphasis found in beginning instruction inculcate a "reader set" as to the nature of the reading act? Specifically, can a child *learn* to over-rely on learning sight words, letter-sound relationships, or use of context clues? Are these skills so unrelated that one should be given priority for a designated period, then another be stressed, etc., or should these be seen as concomitant learnings which complement each other?

Next, there is considerable data on the variability of English spellings and on the frequency with which phonic rules apply to printed words usually met in the primary grades. How is this data translated into classroom practice? Other instructional problems include providing a meaningful differentiation of phonics instruction based on pupil differences, and the selection of a defensible sequence for teaching the myriad of steps in the total phonics program. A discussion of these issues appears to be essential if one is to see phonics instruction in proper perspective.

The "Either-Or" Phenomenon in Phonics Instruction

It is most unfortunate that the relationship between phonics instruction and learning to read has been clouded by debate which has focused attention on a spurious issue. For years this debate was couched in terms which implied that all reading instruction fell into one of two categories—a sight-word method *or* a phonics method. Neither of these methodological polar-positions actually existed in anything like a pure form. However, when reading instruction was discussed within this *either-or* framework, there was a tendency to ignore significant educational issues and simply challenge one or the other extremes.

In the early 1960's this fruitless debate began to subside, primarily because no advocates of a "non-phonics" approach could be found and all available instructional materials provided for teaching phonics. Unfortunately the *sight-word method* vs. *phonics method* controversy was replaced by a very closely related *either-or* polarization.

In Chall's recent book, *Learning To Read — The Great Debate*[1], the author accepts the premise that beginning reading instruction fits

---

[1] *The Great Debate* is discussed here primarily because it seems destined to be influential. Few books on reading methodology have aroused more comment and discussion. An extensive review in *Newsweek* (November 6, 1967) quoted Dr. John W. Gardner, Secretary of Health, Education and Welfare as stating that this book was, "the most important book on education of the past ten years." The Carnegie Corporation, which supported Dr. Chall's study, gave her views wide circulation in *The Carnegie Quarterly* (XV, No. 3, Summer, 1967). The Reading Reform Foundation (a group devoted to early and intensive phonics instruction), suggested in a letter to presidents of colleges and universities which train teachers, "We earnestly beg you to review the courses in reading instruction in your curriculum with Dr. Chall's findings in mind." (Letter, November 27, 1967, signed Watson Washburn). In December, 1967, the same foundation addressed a letter to the governors of the fifty states (enclosing a copy of the *Carnegie Quarterly* which reviewed the book). The following is a quote from one paragraph:

> In view of Professor Chall's verdict on *The Great Debate,* vouched for by Dr. Gardner, and backed by the researchers from 1912 to this date, there is no excuse for further delay.... we earnestly urge that you act immediately to install intensive alphabet-phonic methods and textbooks in all your States' elementary schools, arrange in-service intensive phonic instruction for the teachers (this takes only a few weeks), and direct all teachers' colleges to require for graduation a course in intensive phonics.

comfortably into two categories — one is "meaning emphasis," the other is "code emphasis." These terms are different names for the older *sight-word method* vs. *phonics method*. It is alleged that the conventional wisdom (current practice) and the reading establishment advocate that beginning reading instruction should consist of meaning emphasis; while the author unequivocally recommends code emphasis "as a *beginning* reading method."

In *Learning To Read — The Great Debate,* the author reviews selected studies which compared the effects of different amounts of phonics in the primary grades. She concluded that programs which included systematic phonics instruction resulted in higher pupil achievement than did those programs which included little or no phonics. This conclusion appears wholly justifiable and is consistent with a point of view frequently expressed prior to the publication of *The Great Debate.*

However, the second conclusion and recommendation found in the book invites closer scrutiny. Chall writes:

> In summary, judging from the studies comparing systematic with intrinsic phonics, we can say that systematic phonics *at the very beginning* (emphasis added) tends to produce better reading and spelling achievement than intrinsic phonics, at least through grade 3. (4:114)
>
> My analysis of the existing experimental comparisons of a meaning emphasis versus a code emphasis tends to support Bloomfield's definition that the *first step* (emphasis added) in learning to read in one's native language is essentially learning a printed code for the speech we possess. (4:83)
>
> Nor can I emphasize too strongly that I recommend a code emphasis only as a *beginning* reading method—a method to *start* the child on . . . . (Emphasis appears in original, 4:307.)

The conclusion seems warranted that Dr. Chall does recommend *code emphasis as a beginning reading method.* Furthermore, the author states that this recommendation stems from an analysis of the many studies cited in the text.

A review of the studies cited in *The Great Debate* discloses that the majority of these studies did not deal with the variable of *initial* code cracking versus *initial* meaning instruction. They dealt primarily with the variable of the *amount of phonics* instruction included in grades one and two (and in some cases grade three).

If this analysis is correct it puts the issue of phonics instruction in an entirely different perspective — one need not choose an either-or approach to *beginning reading instruction.* The crucial fact is that beginning reading *must include* code cracking or the teaching of letter-sound relationships. However, research data do not suggest that beginning reading be equated with code cracking.

The reader can find a number of sentences or brief passages in Dr. Chall's book that appear to unequivocally support this latter position. Such statements suggest that the author of *The Great Debate* perceived the fact that the real difference between beginning methods is the *amount of phonics* instruction included, not the fact that code cracking must precede all other instructional procedures.
For example:

A. I cannot stress sufficiently that this dichotomy (code *vs.* meaning) is only one of emphasis. (4: 137)
B. I believe we may chance at least one inference from Gray's case studies: Too little or too much phonics may contribute to failure. (4: 163)

We are in total agreement with these statements, and if these statements should represent the main thrust of *The Great Debate*, there is no quarrel with the book.

However, in the opinion of this writer such redeeming sentences here and there do not represent the main thrust of the book, which is interpreted to be a plea for *code cracking first.* Insofar as this analysis is correct, it invites the reader to again condition his thinking about phonics instruction on an *either-or* basis.

ESSENTIAL CONCOMITANT LEARNINGS

The premise favored in this book is that beginning reading instruction should not consist of *either* code cracking *or* emphasis on meaning without letter-sound analysis. It is doubtful whether reading instruction can ever become as effective as it might be as long as *either* code cracking *or* reading for meaning are presented as alternatives rather than as concomitant learnings. Beginning reading instruction must produce measurable growth on three very closely related fronts. The reader must constantly be:

A. mastering and applying letter-sound relationships
B. enlarging his sight vocabulary
C. profiting from context clues while reading.

The history of reading instruction in American schools has been characterized by a movement from one extreme to another in regard to phonics. From the extreme of code cracking unrelated to *reading* in which pupils drilled on isolated letter sounds; to attempts to teach reading with no code cracking; to gradual code cracking with little or none in initial instruction; to initial reading *is* code cracking.

Educators' behavior in regard to this one problem of phonics appears to border on the instinctive, closely resembling that of the lemmings. While the lemmings take an extreme action at least once every 20 years to *solve* their problem, educators appear to insist on extreme action in order to *preserve* their problem. Many educators, as well as their critics, cannot focus on the issue of phonics or code cracking in beginning reading except in terms of *versus*, *either-or*, or *all or nothing*. There are no extremes on the phonics instruction continuum that have not been advocated, or to which educators will not eventually return. Each return is heralded as a major educational breakthrough.

It is not realistic to devote the first few months of reading instruction to one of the above skills (A, B, C), while ignoring the other two. Such an approach will confuse a child as to the nature of the reading process. Also, it increases the possibility of his learning to *overrely* on one of the three essentials rather than viewing them as always working together.

Overreliance on One Skill Is Not Efficient

If one of the skills (A, B, C above) is overemphasized in beginning reading the child is likely to *overlearn* and *overrely* on this skill. This mitigates against his maintaining a proper balance between these three essentials for growth. The longer he relies more or less exclusively on one skill, the more impaired his reading will become. This is true whether his "set" is for learning sight words, sounding all words, or hypothesizing as to what a word might be from other context clues.

The beginning reader should be receiving instruction which helps him crack the code. However, he is handicapped if he relies too heavily on phonic analysis. If a child *can* and *does* sound every word in a story he is not becoming an efficient reader. He is analyzing some words long after he should have mastered them as sight words. That is, he may be sounding words the tenth, twentieth, or fiftieth time he meets them. Since the objective of reading instruction is not to produce this kind of reader, every effort should be made to see that the child does not generalize that "sounding out words is reading." Conversely, it would be foolish and wasteful to have the child rely solely on learning words as wholes, since he must learn and apply the knowledge that printed letters signal certain speech sounds.

Variability of Letter Sounds in English

One factor which limits the degree to which the reader can rely on phonic analysis is the large number of English words which have irregular spellings. Although written English is alphabetic, the irregular spellings of words prevents anything like a one-to-one relationship between letters seen and sounds heard. Some of the reasons for, and examples of this problem are:

1. Many English words have come from other languages such as Latin, Greek, French, and German (waive, alias, corps, debris, alien, buoy, feint, bouquet, etc.).
2. A given letter, or letters, may have many different sounds in different words (cow [ow]; low [ō]; can [ă]; cane [ā]; cap [k]; city [s]; bus [s]; his [z]; measure [zh]).
3. In thousands of English words, a letter or letters may have no sound (know, kick, listen, light, plumb, wring).

The following examples illustrate some of the variability found in English words. Some words are:

> pronounced the same,
> spelled differently,
> and each is phonetically "lawful."

sail — sale; meat — meet; heal — heel; maid — made

In these examples, the generalization which applies to both spellings is:

> When there are two vowels in a word, usually the first is long and the second is silent.

In the following, one word in each pair is governed by the phonic generalization listed above — the *other* is not.

ate	rain	peace	wait
eight	reign	piece	weight

A word may have one or more *silent letters* which differentiates it from another word which is pronounced exactly the same:

rap	our	no	night	plum
wrap	hour	know	knight	plumb

Some words are spelled exactly the same but have different origins, meanings, and pronunciations.

> "Your mother will *object* if you keep this *object* in your room."
> "The author was *content* with the *content* of his story."

The long sound of vowels may be represented by any of these and other combinations in words:

day	they	fate	sail	reign	great	
$\bar{a}=ay$	*ey*	*a* (e)	*ai*	*ei*	*ea*	
feet	meat	deceive	brief	ski	key	
$\bar{e}=ee$	*ea*	*ei*	*ie*	*i*	*ey*	
my	kite	pie	height	buy	guide	
$\bar{i}=y$	*i* (e)	*ie*	*ei*	*uy*	*ui*	
show	hold	boat	note	go	door	four
$\bar{o}=ow$	*o* (+ld)	*oa*	*o* (e)	*o*	*oo*	*ou*
flew	view	tube	due	suit	you	
$\bar{u}=ew$	*iew*	*u*	*ue*	*ui*	"	

It should be evident from the above that it would not be easy to write a series of rules to cover the sounds that letters represent in English. In fact, there *is no phonic rule* which will apply to all words which meet the criteria the rule sets forth. Therefore, any phonic rule may have to be "amended" many times to cover the situations the original rule was designed to cover. As an example, let us look at the most widely applicable rule relating to vowel sounds:

> A single vowel in medial position, in a word or syllable, usually has its short sound.

This generalization is quite useful to children learning to read. Studies of the frequency with which it applies to words met in primary reading support the view that it should be taught.(5) However, it should also be pointed out that there are a great number of instances in which the generalization does not hold. The following are examples of exceptions followed by generalizations which have emerged to cover these situations.

Exception A:	*hold, cold, bold, gold; bolt, colt.*
New rule:	The single vowel *o*, followed by *ld* or *lt*, has its long sound.
Exception B:	*car, fir, fur, her, for, part, bird, hurt, perch, corn.*
New rule:	A vowel followed by *r* has neither its long nor short sound — the vowel sound is modified by the *r*.

Exception C:	*wild, mild, child; find, kind, mind, blind.*
New rule:	The vowel *i* before *ld* or *nd* is usually long.
Exception D:	*fall, call, ball; salt, malt, halt.*
New rule:	The vowel *a* followed by *ll* or *lt,* has a pronunciation like *aw* (ball = bawl).
Exception E:	*high, sigh; light, night, bright, flight.*
New rule:	The vowel *i* in *igh* or *ight* words is usually long.
Other exceptions:	sign = (i); was = (ō); both = (ō); front = (u).

These illustrations have dealt only with monosyllabic words containing a single vowel in medial position. The "exceptions" to the basic rule are only the major ones which might logically be dealt with in teaching reading, and the words listed represent only a small fraction of those that could be cited. The point of this discussion is not to attempt to refute the premise that "there is ample reason for teaching phonics — and teaching it well," but rather to suggest that phonics has its limitations when applied to learning to read English.

TEACHING RULES FOR SOUNDING

In a number of different sources, one might read that 85 per cent of English words are phonetic. It is not clear what this statement means; but it probably was meant to imply the possibility of formulating enough phonic rules to cover approximately this percentage of English words. As rules become more involved and cover fewer and fewer actual words, one may question the relationship between learning these rules and learning the process called reading.

In recent years, teachers have had considerable data available that focus on the frequency with which various phonic rules apply to words children will meet in their primary and elementary school experiences. Studies by Oaks (7), Clymer (5), Bailey (1), Emans (6), Burmeister (3), Burrows and Lourie (2), are very much in agreement in their findings that there are a significant number of exceptions to generalizations covering vowel sounds.

The educational issue is not arriving at a universally agreed upon list of rules to be taught. The real problem, which is much more complicated, is what happens to learners under various types of instruction which focuses on rules. What types of attack strategies do children develop? There is very little data to guide teachers. Those who have worked extensively with impaired readers have undoubtedly encountered some children who are "rule oriented." Some of these children persist in trying to make the rule *fit* even when the word they are attacking is an exception. Others can cite the rule and are still unable to apply it to words which it covers.

Despite the absence of data which might serve as a guide for teaching phonic generalization, teachers must decide on the teaching strategies they will use. They may choose instructional materials which make a fetish of memorizing phonic generalizations. They might, on the other hand, present a series of words which are governed by a particular rule and invite children to formulate a generalization. The latter course seems preferable not just because it fits under the rubric discovery method, but because it permits the child to work with concepts he can understand. Furthermore, it relieves the learning situation of a certain degree of rigidity and reduces the finality that is usually associated with a rule. However, neither the use of the discovery method nor the memorization of rules changes the facts of English spellings which definitely limits the degree to which phonic analysis can aid the reader.

The Rationale for Learning Whole Words

Even when one starts from the premise that a child *must* learn to associate printed letter symbols with speech sounds, this does not negate the fact that one must also learn to recognize whole words. Whenever a child is making normal progress in learning to read, he is increasing his sight vocabulary or stock of words which he recognizes instantly. At the end of grade one he will have a larger sight vocabulary than at the end of five months of instruction and practice. At the conclusion of grade two his sight vocabulary will be much larger than it was at the beginning of that school year. The skill that best illustrates the developmental nature of reading is the acquisition of a sight vocabulary. When the reader meets words he recognizes, he does not apply phonic analysis. He knows what spoken word the printed form represents, so there is nothing to solve through letter-sound analysis.

Also, as noted above, the irregular spellings of many English words precludes the application of phonic analysis and dictates that these words be learned as sight words. In addition, there are a number of words which appear so frequently in English speech and writing that it would be very wasteful to sound out these words each time they are met. For example, after only a few weeks of reading instruction, which centers on normal English usage, a child will have met each of the following words often: *the, was, could, any, been, do, head, give, great, have, many, love, does, one, done, here, of, said, too, use, very, gone, should, who, some, put, move, none, son, two, were, what, know, live, once, sure, their.* Each of these words represent an irregular spelling. Yet, these and some 200 other words occur in English speech and writing with exceptionally high frequency. They have been labeled glue words, sight words, or structure words.

For a period of time which spanned the 1940's and early 1950's one could find suggestions that the beginning reader learn 50-75-100 sight words before letter-sound analysis was introduced. Such a practice undoubtedly overemphasized learning sight words and postponed longer than necessary the introduction of systematic phonics instruction. When one learns both sight words and letter-sound analysis as part of his on-going instruction, he sees these skills in proper perspective. While it may be impossible to prevent a few children from overrelying on one or the other skill, it is possible not to deliberately teach them to do so.

There are a number of reasons which have frequently been cited as justification for teaching and learning some whole words as units during the early stages of reading instruction. These are briefly summarized below.

1. The child's knowledge of, and use of, oral language involves the meaningful use of words and of words in combination. We wish the learner to move one short step from what is known to what is to be learned. Reading is a more meaningful process when the child deals with whole words as units, rather than working exclusively with letter sounds. Meaning resides in the total word and in the special ways words are used together not in the sound of the individual letter-parts of words. This does not preclude working with both words and letter-sound analysis in the same lesson.

2. Spoken language and printed word symbols maintain a one-to-one relationship, regardless of the gross spelling irregularities found in English. However, the sounds contributed by individual letters in printed words vary tremendously.

3. If a child knows a number of words as sight words, he can more easily be taught to see and hear similarities between the known words and new words he meets.

4. Many words met in beginning reading do not lend themselves to phonic analysis. These should be learned as sight words.

5. The objective of reading instruction is not to have the child analyze each word. However, if in beginning instruction he is taught only to analyze words, this habit will be acquired.

6. Learning whole words teaches children to look at the whole word from left to right, as opposed to some phonic systems which advocate

teaching vowel sounds first. In a vast majority of words, this mode of attack will start the analysis in the middle of words, rather than at the beginning of the word.

The Sequence in Which Phonic Skills Are Taught

There are many questions relative to the sequence of teaching phonics skills which are of minor consequence. Examples include: the order in which consonant sounds or consonant blends are taught; should vowel sounds be taught in the order they appear in the alphabet; should long vowel sounds be taught first or short vowel sounds, or both together to emphasize the contrast?

The question of whether to introduce the teaching of phonics by teaching consonant sounds first or vowel sounds first is worthy of some discussion. There is little question that children can learn these skills in either order. The questions which teachers should answer are:

1. What are the data related to the issue of teaching consonant or vowel sounds first?

2. Are the procedures which I follow supported by sound learning theory?

The following discussion examines a number of the justifications commonly advanced by proponents of teaching consonant sounds first and by those who support teaching vowel sounds first.

Rationale for Teaching Consonant Sounds First. 1. The majority of words children meet in beginning reading are words which begin with consonants. For instance, 175 (or approximately 80 per cent) of the 220 words on the Dolch Basic Sight Word Test[2] begin with consonants. The Dale List of 769 Easy Words[3] contains even a higher proportion (87 per cent) of words beginning with consonants.

2. It is good learning theory to have the child start phonic analysis with the beginning of words, working his way through the words from left to right. This reinforces the practice of reading from left to right and focuses the child's attention on the first part of the word. This is essential for facile reading, and an absolute prerequisite if he is to solve the word by sounding. (See related discussion, pp. 7–8, 19–20.)

3. Consonants tend to be much more consistent than vowels in sound representation. For instance, a number of consonants (j, k, l, m, n, p, b, h, r, v, w) represent only one sound. Certain other

---

[2] Obtainable from The Garrard Press, Champaign, Illinois.

[3] Edgar Dale, "A Comparison of Two Word Lists," *Educational Research Bulletin*, December 9, 1931, pp. 484–89.

consonants which have two sounds present no problem in *beginning* reading instruction because one of the two basic sounds can be left until the child has had some considerable practice in reading. Examples:

> c=k in cat, cake, color, cup, cap, cut, could, can, cold, cry, call, clean, cage
>
> c=s when c is followed by e, i, or y (cent, century, ceiling, cypress, celebrate, citizen, cycle, cease)
>
> d has d sound in did, doll, don't, day, do, dog, dish
>
> d has j sound in individual, graduate, cordial

4. If a child uses skills in combination, sounding the initial letter which is usually a consonant, and using context-meaning clues, will frequently be all the analysis that is needed. Assume each blank line in the following illustrations represents an unknown word.

> 1. _____ (This could represent *any* of 600,000 words in English)
> 2. f_____ (Here, more than 95 per cent of all words are eliminated. The unknown word *must* begin with the sound associated with the letter *f*.)

It is probable that the reader will arrive at the unknown word(s) in the following sentences despite the very limited context which is provided.

> 3. You will have to pay the f_____ now, said the judge.
> 4. Without a doubt, pumpkin is my f_____ pie.
> 5. He took the stolen jewels to the f_____.
> 6. During J_____ it is much colder than it is in J_____ and J_____.

Rationale for Teaching Vowel Sounds First. 1. Beginning readers can learn to associate the printed vowel letters with the speech sounds they represent. The more quickly they learn these associations the more quickly they will become independent readers. This statement is equally valid when applied to consonant letter-sound associations. However, it does not provide justification for teaching either vowel or consonant association first.

2. Beginning phonic analysis with vowel sounds, it is stated, is justifiable because vowels carry more of a clue to the word's pronunciation than do consonants. If this is true, it is indeed a crucial reason

for teaching vowel letter-sound associations first. However, there is no evidence which supports the statement.[4] Assume the following blank space represents a missing vowel: 1—ck. There are only four possibilities—lack, lick, lock, luck. Insert each of these vowels, but leave the initial consonant blank and a much larger number of possibilities results:

-ack	-ick	-ock	-uck
back	Dick	cock	buck
hack	kick	dock	duck
Jack	hick	lock	huck
lack	lick	mock	luck
Mack	pick	rock	muck
pack	sick	sock	puck
rack	tick		suck
sack	wick		tuck

The same holds true for double vowels:

-eed can be	seed	weed	need	reed	deed	feed	heed
-eat can be	meat	heat	neat	peat	seat	feat	beat
-ail can be	tail	mail	bail	fail	pail	rail	nail

Paul McKee, who was worked extensively with beginning readers on all facets of word analysis writes: ". . . time and time again the author has found that in reading connected discourse first-grade pupils can unlock strange words easily without knowing any of the letter-sound associations represented by vowels in these words. . . . Parenthetically, it should be added that these first-grade pupils had no trouble reading an unfamiliar primer story in which all the words included were familiar to them in print and a blank was substituted for each vowel sound in each word."[5]

3. Vowels should be taught first because all words and syllables contain vowels.

If the words *a, I,* and *eye* are eliminated one may demonstrate that all words also contain consonants. How the fact that all words contain vowels is a justification for teaching vowel sounds first has not been explained in any material which has come to the writer's attention.

In summary, it would appear that certain facts — (1) consonants are consistent in their sound; (2) the vast majority of words begin

---

[4] See William S. Gray, *On Their Own in Reading* (Chicago: Scott, Foresman & Company, 1960), pp. 35–36.

[5] Paul McKee, *Reading, a Program of Instruction for the Elementary School* (Boston: Houghton Mifflin Company, 1966), p. 104.

with consonants; (3) children should learn to read English from left to right and analyze words left to right — offer a substantial basis for teaching consonants first.

Differentiation of Instruction

What we know about children and how they learn would dictate that we accept the premise that all children in a given classroom do not need identical amounts of phonic instruction. Most phonics instruction materials do not make provision for pupil differences. Differentiation of instruction in this area is primarily the task of the teacher, just as it is in all areas of the curriculum.

To provide less instruction than a child *needs* would deny him the opportunity to master a skill that he *must have* in order to progress in independent reading. To subject other children to drill they do not need runs the risk of destroying interest in the act of reading. It is a simple matter to turn off a potential learner by requiring that he sit through group drill on sounding letters; or complete a series of workbook pages which force him to deal with minute details of word attack when he is already capable of applying these skills in sustained reading.

The key to providing children with what they need in the way of instruction is knowledge of their weaknesses. This knowledge is acquired through diagnosis. The best diagnosis is observation and analysis of *reading behavior*. It would seem that discovering what a child needs in the area of code cracking ability should be relatively easy, since he cannot help but disclose his needs. Every technique he might use to cover his weakness is an added clue. Some of the more obvious behaviors are omitting, miscalling, or substituting words.

Listening to a child read a sentence or two should provide the teacher with clues to his word attack ability. A hypothesis that a particular skill is lacking can be tested by having the child read words or sentences containing words which call for him to make the letter-sound relationships which fit the hypothesis. If this simple informal test discloses a problem, the teacher selects or develops appropriate materials, and works simultaneously with all pupils who can profit from the instruction she has decided upon.

PRINCIPLES TO APPLY IN TEACHING PHONICS

The systematic study of any teaching-learning situation may be expected to yield a set of psychologically sound principles which relate to and govern teaching procedures. In teaching, one would follow sound principles in order to enhance learning. Principles do not spell out precise practices to be followed, but rather provide a set of guidelines by which to measure classroom instructional practices. The following principles for teaching phonic analysis are advanced for teachers' consideration. If these principles are found to be educationally sound, they merit application in the classroom.

1. *For any child to profit from systematic phonics instruction he must be able to discriminate between different speech sounds in words; and visually discriminate between printed letters.* The absence of either of these prerequisites would preclude learning letter-sound relationships. For example, a child who can differentiate between the sounds of bee and dee, but cannot visually discriminate between the printed symbols b and d cannot apply phonics in a reading situation which involves words containing these symbols.

2. *Practices followed in beginning reading DO tend to inculcate a "set" in the learner.* Instruction should not lead the child to think of reading as consisting of *either* learning sight words, *or* sounding letters, *or* relying on context clues. Such instruction is likely to result in over-reliance on one or another of these essential skills.

3. *Instructional practice which leads to over reliance on one method of word attack is indefensible.* In any reading situation, words appear in context; some words will be met very frequently and should gradually be learned as units; and some words will have to be solved through letter-sound analysis. Over reliance on one skill while ignoring all others would be wasteful, and would inhibit the development of facile reading.

4. *All necessary phonic skills (letter-sound relationships) needed by the child to become an independent reader should be taught.*

5. *All elementary teachers should be familiar with the entire phonics program.* All teachers of reading, regardless of grade level, will probably find it necessary to teach, review, or reteach certain phonic skills to some children in their classrooms. Thus, familiarity with all steps in phonics instruction is essential.

6. *All children do not need the same amount of phonics instruction.* The *optimum* amount of phonics instruction for each child is the *minimum* that will result in his becoming an independent reader.

7. *Diagnosis is essential for discovering each child's present needs and diagnosis is the basis for differentiation of instruction.*

8. *The spelling patterns found in English writing limits the usefulness of certain rules or generalizations.* Little value may reside in teaching a generalization which applies to only a few words, or to which exceptions are extremely numerous.

9. *A child's ability to recite phonic generalizations does not assure that he has the ability to apply these generalizations in reading situations.* Some children can recite a given rule and yet have no ability to apply or practice what it tells them to do. On the other hand, knowledge of phonic generalizations is useful to children. In general, material should be presented in such a way that the application of a given generalization evolves out of actual word study. At best, phonic generalizations are a crutch which may have utility at certain points on the learning continuum. A reader who is continually groping for a rule to apply when he meets a word not known as a sight word is not a facile reader.

STEPS IN TEACHING PHONICS

The outline below lists the steps in the order in which they are discussed in the following chapters.

1. Auditory-visual discrimination
2. Teaching consonant sounds
    a) Initial consonants
    b) Consonant digraphs (sh, wh, th, ch)
    c) Consonant blends (br, cl, str, etc.)
    d) Substituting initial consonant sounds
    e) Sounding consonants at end of words
    f) Consonant digraphs (nk, ng, ck, qu)
    g) Consonant irregularities
    h) Silent consonants
    i) Sight-word list — non-phonic spellings
    j) Contractions
3. Teaching vowel sounds
    a) Short vowel sounds
    b) Long vowel sounds
    c) Teaching long and short sounds together
    d) Exceptions to vowel rules taught
    e) Diphthongs
    f) Sounds of $\overline{oo}$ and $\breve{oo}$
4. Syllabication
    a) Rules
    b) Prefixes and suffixes
    c) Compound words
    d) Doubling final consonants
    e) Accent

These steps in phonic analysis represent a series of instructional tasks which merit inclusion in reading instruction. It is suggested that these steps be taught in the order in which they are presented. This is believed to be a logical sequence, but it is not implied that this is the only defensible sequence.

It will be noted that the steps listed are only a bare outline of major facets of instruction. For instance, teaching consonant sounds is one step, but it involves at least two-dozen separate teachings (since some consonants have more than one sound). Teaching consonant digraphs and blends would include another thirty separate tasks. All steps must be reviewed and retaught as needed. Diagnosis of individual pupils' progress will determine when, and how much, review is necessary.

References

(1) Bailey, Mildred Hart, "The Utility of Phonic Generalizations in Grades One Through Six," *Reading Teacher*, 20 (February, 1967) 413–18.

(2) Burroughs, Alvina and Zyra Lourie, "Two Vowels Go Walking," *Reading Teacher*, 17 (November, 1963) 79–82.

(3) Burmeister, Lou E., "Vowel Pairs," *Reading Teacher*, 21 (February, 1968) 445–52.

(4) Chall, Jeanne, *Learning To Read—The Great Debate*. New York: McGraw-Hill Book Company, 1967.

(5) Clymer, Theodore, "The Utility of Phonic Generalizations in The Primary Grades," *Reading Teacher*, 16 (January, 1963) 252–58.

(6) Emans, Robert, "The Usefulness of Phonic Generalizations Above the Primary Grades," *Reading Teacher*, 20 (February, 1967) 419–25.

(7) Oaks, Ruth E., "A Study of the Vowel Situations in a Primary Vocabulary," *Education*, LXXII (May, 1952) 604–17.

Chapter 2

Teaching Auditory-Visual Discrimination and Association of Consonant Letter-Sounds

PHONICS INSTRUCTION RELATED TO PREVIOUS LEARNINGS

Learning to read involves both the ability to make finer and finer visual discriminations between printed word symbols which are very much alike, and the association of oral speech sounds with printed letters and letter combinations. These are often referred to as "mechanical" skills in the reading process and are sometimes contrasted with "comprehension" skills. To establish such a dichotomy may be convenient in a discussion of reading, but it should not be forgotten that no reading can take place in the absence of the discrimination skills just mentioned. Fortunately, the child, before beginning to read, has had many experiences which bear directly on this important learning task.

The most important of these previous experiences deals with language usage. The child upon entering school:

1. can differentiate between thousands of words when he hears them spoken by other individuals
2. can use thousands of words in his own speech
3. has concepts for thousands of words.

These are the language skills which are related to learning to read. Two new skills must be developed — visual recognition of printed words, and association of known speech sounds with printed letters and letter combinations. The following material illustrates a number of approaches for teaching or developing auditory and visual discrimination.

TEACHING AUDITORY DISCRIMINATION

Premise: The successful teaching of all subsequent steps in phonic analysis is based on the child's ability to discriminate between speech sounds in words. The ability to make or use all English speech sounds in words does not assure the ability to discriminate between individual phonemes in words. Children learn spoken words as global units and can easily distinguish between words with minimal phoneme differences. Phonics instruction aims at instant association of a particular sound with a given letter or letters. Thus, if a child cannot distinguish the minute auditory differences being taught in a particular phonics lesson, he cannot profit from that instruction.

Occasionally, children are fairly successful in learning consonant sounds but have trouble in mastering certain vowel sounds. An example of such a case is a high-school student who could not differentiate between spoken words containing the short sound of *e* or *i*. Pairs of words, which differed only as to the vowel in medial position, were numbered for identification purposes. The tutor would say one of the words and ask the boy to give the number of the word pronounced. His responses demonstrated conclusively that he could not aurally distinguish between words such as the following:

A.	(1) bet	(2) bit		D.	(1) pen	(2) pin
B.	(1) Ben	(2) bin		E.	(1) bed	(2) bid
C.	(1) mitt	(2) met		F.	(1) then	(2) thin

Many hours of practice were required for this boy to overcome this deficiency. A tape recorder was used as the tutor and boy read words from identical lists. The tutor would pronounce a word, then the boy would say the same word using the tutor's pronunciation as a model. The student listened to the recordings many times before he was able to differentiate between these vowel sounds.

A learning problem like this could develop because the student could correctly pronounce the words he used in his speech; and he always had context clues when others used words which contained the troublesome sounds. Probably none of his teachers were aware that he still persisted in hearing many words or syllables globally rather than clearly distinguishing component phonemes. To illustrate, if someone clearly spoke the sentence, "The pig is in the PEG PIN," he would be under the impression he had heard, "The pig is in the *pig pen*" because the context seemed to demand this.

The procedures which a teacher might use in helping children develop skill in auditory discrimination are practically unlimited. The following are illustrative:

1. Children listen while the teacher pronounces a series of words, all of which begin with the same consonant sound: belt, ball, bird, be, bone. Children then volunteer other words which begin with the same sound: baby, bug, bat, boom, bang.

2. A number of pictures are collected from workbooks, catalogues, or magazines. Paste each picture on a separate piece of cardboard to make handling easier. The child is to arrange these into groups on the basis of the initial sound of the *name* of the objects pictured. That is, pictures of baby, ball, boat, are put in one group; pictures of house, hand, horse, in another.

3. "What sound do we hear?"

   a) Secure a number of pictures of objects with which children characteristically associate particular sounds.
   b) Paste each picture on a separate piece of cardboard.
   c) As each picture is shown, ask a selected child, or the group, "to make the sound that this object makes." (See Figure 1.)

Figure 1

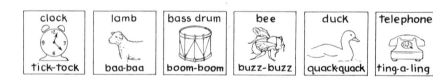

4. Practice in hearing like sounds which conclude words (rhymes).

   a) Teacher pronounces two words.
   b) If the words rhyme (mill—hill), the children clap their hands once. If the words do not rhyme (make—milk), children say "no."

   drum—hum; boom—bang; cap—mad; bake—cake; small—tall; fan—man; sit—hit; cold—gold

5. Children *name* three or four pictures in a group and draw a line connecting those pictures whose names rhyme: (See Figure 2.)

Figure 2

 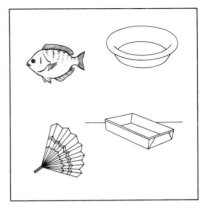

6. Children name a stimulus picture, then circle the word which rhymes with the picture name. (The child must be able to read or sound out the words presented.) The picture stimulus eliminates the possibility of the child relying exclusively on visual clues in matching "words that rhyme".(See Figure 3.)

Figure 3

7. Secure pictures which contain many objects (advertisements, etc.).

> TEACHER: "Do you see an object which begins with the sound we hear at the beginning of the names Billy and Betty?"
>
> (ball—basket)
>
> "Do you see a picture of something which begins with the sound we hear at the beginning of the words hand and help?"
>
> (hat—horse)
>
> Continue to use stimulus words whose initial sound matches that of naming words for objects pictured.

TEACHING VISUAL DISCRIMINATION

Teaching the association of the sound of letters and combination of letters with the printed symbol equivalents is dependent on the child's ability to recognize and discriminate visually between printed letters, such as: "*bad*"—"*dad;*" "*moon*"—"*noon;*" "*bat*"—"*bit*"—"*but*"—"*bet*" Illustrative examples of teaching visual discrimination in reading situations follow:

1. Provide the child with practice in *seeing* identical letter patterns in different words.

    a) *b*all, *b*aby, *b*ird, *b*elt

       "What do you see at the beginning of each of these words?" "Yes, they all begin the same — with the letter *b*. Look at the word closely and LISTEN to the sound of *b* at the beginning of each word." (Pronounce words slowly — moving from left to right.)

    b) h*all*, c*all*, f*all*, t*all*

       (Call attention to visual pattern at the end of each word — pronounce and listen to the sound.)

    c) *bl*ack, *bl*ock, *bl*ue, *bl*ow

       (Have the child note the visual pattern of the two-letter blend, and listen carefully to the sound the letters represent at the beginning of each printed word. Many teachers prefer not to teach a given blend until both letter-sounds involved have been introduced.)

2. Mark each word that begins with the same letter(s) that are underlined in the first word.

make:	move	after	must	lake
tall:	make	take	best	took
block:	laugh	blow	farm	blue
change:	child	came	chair	could
show:	stage	shine	short	year

3. In the following exercise, the teacher reads the sentences. The child should know the letter-name and sound of the stimulus letters *b* and *m*. Children provide the missing words from context plus the initial-letter clue.

    "Children read b_____."

    "Boys play   b_____."

    "Cats like   m_____."

    "Milk costs   m_____."

4. Match words with beginning sound of pictured items (Figure 4):
"Underline the words which begin with the same sound as the picture
object."

Figure 4

The preceding discussion points up the fact that auditory discrimination can be taught before children attempt to read. However,
auditory discrimination in a reading situation is inevitably tied to
visual recognition of letter symbols. Therefore, auditory-visual skills
should be practiced simultaneously.

TEACHING CONSONANT SOUNDS

The following points briefly restate the rationale for teaching consonant sounds before vowel sounds.

1. The majority of words children meet in beginning reading start
with consonants.

2. It is desirable that children learning to read look at the beginning
of a word first; therefore, if phonic analysis is necessary, it should begin
with the first part of the word.

3. The consonant sounds are much more constant than vowel
sounds. When children learn the sound of a given consonant, this sound
will "hold" in most words the child meets.

4. In many instances the context, plus the initial sound (or initial
syllable) of an unknown word will be all the analysis the child will
need to solve the word.

Assuming the child has learned a few sight words, he will know
some printed word symbols which begin with a given consonant. The
first consonant sounds taught might be those which have only one
sound such as *b, r, d, c, s, g, t*. While the order in which consonant

sounds are taught is not of crucial importance, logic might suggest that z, x, q; $c = s$; $g = j$; etc., might be reserved for later teaching.

Consonants in Initial Position

For the purposes of illustration, the steps in teaching the sound of the consonant *b* are given in detail. All other consonant sounds may be taught in the same manner.

a) Print the letter *b* (upper and lower case) on the chalkboard. Indicate that for the next few minutes the group will study the sound

Approach 1

of the letter *b*, as heard in words. Write on the board a column of previously studied words, all of which begin with the letter *b*.

b) Any words the children have met (as sight words) in experience charts or other materials may be used — words such as *baby, ball, be, boy* — also, familiar names of children in the class — *Betty, Billy*, etc. — which call for capital letters.

c) Ask the children to look at the words carefully and name the letter that begins each word. Indicate that a big *B* or capital letter is used in names.

d) As the teacher pronounces the words, the children are asked to *listen* to the sound heard at the beginning of each word. The initial sound is emphasized but not distorted.

e) The children are then invited to read the words in unison, listening carefully to the sound of *b* as they say the words.

f) Ask children to supply other words which begin with the sound of *b* as heard in "*baby*," "*ball*," etc. (Accept any words which begin with *b* — even words with the initial blend sounds as in blue, blow, brown, etc. You may not wish to add the blend words to the list on the board, but you may add others such as book, box, both, buy, but, bat, basket.)

g) Children have not been asked to ISOLATE and sound the letter *b* as *buh*. They hear the sound of *b* as it occurs in words. The word *bat* is not sounded out *buh-ah-tuh = bat*. The word *bat* is a one-syllable, not a three-syllable, word. Emphasis is justifiable — distortion is not.

h) Feel free to vary the above procedures (a–f) in any way that appears to hold promise for enhancing children's learning.

Approach 2

Drill on discrimination may be accomplished through the use of pictures. Assume preliminary board work (as illustrated above) has introduced the sounds of *b*, hard *c*, and *f*. A number of pictures may be secured from magazines, catalogues, and workbooks. Each picture may be pasted on cardboard or oak tag for easier handling. One stimulus picture for each of the initial sounds of *b*, *c*, *f* is selected (book, cat,

Figure 5

fish). Children place all of the pictures which begin with a given sound into piles, boxes, or envelopes. (See Figure 5 for examples of stimulus pictures.)

It will be noted in Approach 2 that the child does not have visual clues provided by the initial letter of printed words (*b*ell, *b*oat, *b*ear, *b*ed, *b*all). He must *pronounce* the name of the pictured object and *hear* the initial sound. Many exercises which purport to exercise or test auditory discrimination can be worked successfully by relying entirely on visual cues. Figure 6 is such an exercise. A picture of a familiar object is shown along with the name of the object (bird).

The child is to underline all of the words which begin with the same *sound* as the stimulus word and pictured object. This exercise is useful only if the child actually "sounds out" and listens carefully to the initial sound heard in each instance. If he simply recognizes *visually* that *b*aby starts with the same letter as *b*ird, he may do the exercise correctly, yet receive no practice in auditory discrimination.

To avoid undesirable repetition, the step-by-step teaching of other initial consonants will not be presented. A list of easier words which might be used in board work for teaching each of the other consonant sounds is presented in Table 5 at the end of this chapter. As long as the initial sound is constant the words used for illustrative purposes do not need to be phonetic throughout — many are sight words.

Figure 6

Teaching Consonant Digraphs (sh, wh, th, ch)

Digraphs are combinations of two letters which result in one speech sound. The sound heard is not a blend of the two letters involved, but is a completely new sound. A given digraph may have more than one pronunciation but the letter combination results in a single sound in each case (*ch = k* in "*ch*orus;" *sh* in "*ch*ef;" *ch* in "*ch*urch"). Digraphs may be taught in a manner similar to that used for teaching consonant sounds.

```
SHALL

SHE

SHIP

SHOW
```

Steps in Brief

1. Place several stimulus words on the chalkboard.
2. Ask the children to look at the words carefully and note how they are alike. Draw out the observation that all words begin with *sh*. (Underline the digraph being taught; i.e., *sh, ch, th, wh*.)
3. Ask the children to listen to the sound of *sh* as they say the words together.
4. Invite children to supply other words which begin with the same sound as "*sh*all," "*sh*e," "*sh*ip," "*sh*ow."

NOTE: The digraph *sh* usually has the sound heard in these stimulus words. Other common *sh* words:

shut, shop, shot, sheep, shape, shade, short, sheet, shoot, shoe, shell, shirt, shovel, shake, sharp, shine
Words ending with *sh* sounds: push, dish, wish, wash.

wh. The digraph *wh* is usually pronounced as if spelled *hw*: when = hwen; white = hwite. The *wh* sound may be taught as is *sh* above. Other common *wh* words: why, where, wheel, wheat, whisper, whether, whale, whiskers.

```
WHEN
WHITE
WHAT
WHICH
```

Exceptions: When *o* follows *wh*, the *w* is silent: who = ho͞o; whole = hōl; whom = ho͞om; whose = ho͞oz.

(Changing patterns of pronunciation will likely find some dictionaries recognizing a second pronunciation: When = wĕn).

th. The digraph *th* has two common sounds. (The concepts of *voiced* and *unvoiced* need not be taught in relation to reading).

Voiced th sound as in:					*Unvoiced th sound as in:*			
this	their	they	though		thing	thin	thimble	thank
that	then	there	than	them	think	thick	third	thumb

ch. While the consonant digraph *ch* has three different sounds, the most common and the one met almost exclusively in beginning reading is that of *ch* heard in *chair* or *much*:

(Common words for use in teaching exercises)

chair	chin	chose	charm	chalk	each	reach
child	check	chop	chance	cheer	such	church
chicken	cheek	change	chimney	chief	watch	much

Much later, children will meet the other sounds represented by *ch*. These need not be taught in beginning reading.

ch = k		*ch = sh*	
chorus	(ko rus)	chef	(shef)
character	(kar ak ter)	chassis	(shas ĭ)
chemist	(kem ist)	chauffeur	(sho fur)
choir	(kwir)	chic	(shek)
chord	(kord)	chiffon	(shif on)
chrome	(krom)	chamois	(sham ĭ)

Teaching Consonant Blends

Consonant blends consist of two or more letters which are blended when pronouncing the word. If a child attempts to sound separately each of the consonants in a blend, distortion and confusion will result. These letters must be blended to arrive at the correct sound. The child *knows these speech sounds* — he must learn to recognize their printed equivalents. For example, the pupil knows the sound of *s*, as heard in *see, sit, some, say*; and the sound of *t*, as heard in *tell, to talk, top*. The next short step, from the known to the unknown, would be teaching the blend sound *st*, as heard in *stop, still, stand*, and the like.

Two- and three-letter consonant blends may be divided into three major groups on the basis of a common letter:

1. Those in which *r* is the concluding letter (see Column *A*).
2. Those in which *l* is the concluding letter (see Column *B*).

3. Those which begin with the letter *s* (see Column *C*).

Column A		Column B		Column C	
br	scr	bl	spl	sc	str
cr	spr	cl		sk	
dr	str	fl		sm	
fr	thr	gl		sn	
gr		pl		sp	
pr		sl		st	
tr				sw	

The above are arranged in alphabetical order, but may be taught in any order desired. The two-letter blends are easier to learn and occur more frequently in words met in beginning reading than do the three-letter blends. Therefore, the former are taught first.

There are a number of ways to teach children how to master these blend sounds. Regardless of the approach used, the objectives in teaching blends are to have the child:

1. *see* the letter combination involved
2. realize that in every case the letters combine into a blend sound
3. discriminate between the blend sound and the sound of individual letters, i.e., "*pay,* "*lay*," "*play.*"

Procedures used in teaching initial blends closely parallel those used in teaching initial consonant sounds. For illustrative purposes the steps in teaching the sound represented by *st* are given in detail (see Procedure A below). All other consonant blends may be taught in the same manner. Exercises which provide drill on auditory-visual recognition of blends are illustrated in Procedure B.

Procedure A

```
STOP
STILL
STAR
STAND
STICK
```

a) Place a few *st* words on the board.

b) Children are asked to look at each word, and attention is directed to the *st* beginning.

c) As the teacher pronounces each word, the pupils are asked to listen to the sound the *st* makes in each word. The words should be pronounced clearly with emphasis on the initial blend sound.

d) The manner in which the *s* and *t* are blended into one sound is emphasized. The sound is the one heard at the beginning of the words *stop*, *still*, *star*.

e) Children may be asked to give other words which begin with this sound. (See Table 6). Accept all words given which have the *st* combination. Write any or all suggested words beneath the stimulus words already on the board.

f) Various pupils may go to the board and underline the two letters (st) as they pronounce the words *stop*, *still*, etc.

Providing Drill on Visual-auditory Recognition of Blends

Procedure B

After teaching several consonant blends, provide further practice through board work or teacher-made seat-work exercises. (Examples of such exercises are shown below.)

a) Prepare a series of three stimulus words. The teacher pronounces one of the words in each series. Children listen and underline the word the teacher pronounces.

1. blue	2. front	3. *drum*	4. *second*	5. friend
blow	friend	dear	small	family
brake	*farm*	drink	smart	*fright*

6. plant	7. smile	8. black	9. plain	10. dress
plank	smell	*plank*	*plant*	dive
paint	*sailed*	blank	party	*drive*

b) Spell a word correctly by filling in the missing spaces with the blends: fl, st, fr, tr:

– – ain	– – eet	– – esh	– – our	– – oor
– – ake	– – ill	– – are	– – orm	– – ibe
– – uff	– – eeze	– – eat	– – all	– – ost

c) Add one of the letters *b*, *f*, *p*, *s* in front of each word to produce a consonant blend at the beginning of each word. Pronounce the word and underline the consonant blend:

– rock	– kill	– lay	– rain	– take
– kit	– lot	– right	– tar	– late
– lump	– ranch	– tack	– lock	– rag
– rake	– lace	– top	– room	– lip

d) Underline all of the beginning consonant blends in the following sentences. (Italics not provided on pupil's worksheet.)

1. Jane bought a *st*ory book at the *st*ore.
2. *Pl*ease, may I *pl*ay when I *cl*ean off my *pl*ate?
3. *Sm*art boys *dr*ink *fr*esh milk *fr*om the farm.
4. *Sm*itty *tr*aded his *dr*um for a book full of *st*amps.

A list of easier consonant-blend words which might be used board- or seat-work exercises is found in Table 6 at the end of this chapter.

Substitution of Initial Consonant Sounds

Day by day, in the early stages of reading instruction, the child is learning both *sight words* and the *sounds* of initial consonants. Knowledge thus gained can be applied in arriving at the pronunciation of other words not known as sight words. Assume the child knows the words *king* and *ring*, and meets the unknown word *sing*. He should be able to combine the *s* sound, which he knows in words like *sat*, *some*, or *say*, with the sound of *ing* found in *king* and *ring*. This involves a process of "thinking the sounds."[1]

For illustrative purposes, let us assume that:

1. a child has learned the italicized words in Table 1,

2. he has learned the sound of the initial consonant as heard in these italicized words,

3. he has not met or learned any of the other thirty-five words in Table 1,

Table 1

bat	*can*	*fit*	*had*	*map*	*pet*	*run*	*say*
cat	ban	bit	bad	cap	bet	bun	bay
fat	fan	hit	fad	rap	met	fun	hay
hat	man	pit	mad	sap	set	sun	may
mat	pan	sit	pad				pay
pat	ran		sad				ray
rat							

---

[1] For a further discussion of this principle, see William S. Gray, *On Their Own in Reading.*

4. by using his knowledge, plus some guidance from the teacher, he should be able to sound out all of the words in Table 1.

By the process of "thinking the sound" of any known consonant and blending this sound with the phonogram which concludes a known sight word, the child should be able to pronounce the new word.

1. Place a known word on the board.   bat

2. Have the children observe closely as the initial *b* is erased,   – at
and a different known consonant is substituted.   cat

3. Follow the same procedure, substituting other consonants
to make easy words.

*f*at	*m*at
*h*at	*r*at

For convenience in building mental substitution exercises, Table 7 provides a series of "word families." In each of these, the words end in a common phonogram (*et, ick, ack, ay, op, un, ill, am, ug, ed,* etc.). Not all words cited need be used in beginning reading, and those beginning with blends should not be used in substitution exercises until the sounds of these blends have been taught.

Sounding Consonants at End of Words

The sounds of the various consonants have been taught as they occur at the beginning of words. The same procedures may be used for teaching children to *hear* these sounds at the end of words. Teaching one final consonant sound (t) is illustrated.

1. Place stimulus words on board.

2. Call children's attention to final letter.

3. Pronounce each word carefully, so that children hear the sound at the end of the word.

4. Have children pronounce words — and supply others which end with this sound.

Stimulus words which might be used in board- or seat-work exercises:

b	d	f	g	k (ck)	l (ll)	m
Bob	sad	if	dog	back	call	him
tub	fed	calf	big	rock	tell	room
club	send	muff	flag	black	hill	gum
grab	glad	stiff	rug	trick	pull	ham
rob	cold	puff	drug	duck	still	whom
rib	band	off	bag	pick	small	drum

n	p	r	s (s)	s (=z)	t
can	hop	for	bus	his	cat
win	cap	star	yes	as	met
men	stop	her	dress	ours	shut
thin	up	dear	us	is	hit
when	step	door	less	has	set
ran	skip	clear	likes	runs	sat
moon	map	car	miss	days	but

Teaching Consonant Blends and Digraphs at End of Words

1. The *sounds* of these letter combinations will have been taught as they occur at the beginning of words.

2. Procedures for teaching these sounds at the end of words may parallel those used for teaching initial sounds.

   a) Place stimulus words on board.

   b) Have children "see" the letter combinations under discussion.

   c) Pronounce each word carefully so children *hear* sound at end of word.

   d) Have children pronounce words.

Stimulus words (ending with common blends and digraphs) which might be used in board- or seat-work exercises:

march	fish	tenth	must	ask	crisp
church	cash	both	fast	desk	grasp
peach	fresh	north	rest	brisk	clasp
branch	rush	bath	coast	task	wisp
ditch	crash	health	most	dusk	rasp
search	dish	path	last	risk	
beach	flash	length	best	mask	
patch	wish	fifth	toast	tusk	
bench	push	cloth	chest	flask	

Consonant Digraphs (nk, ng, ck, qu)

Teaching *nk, ng, ck,* involves associating these letter combinations at the end of words or syllables with the sounds they represent. These digraphs may be taught as follows:

NK   "The sound of NK at the end of words is the sound we hear in these words."

bank	link	junk
rank	mink	sunk
sank	pink	drunk
tank	sink	shrunk

Other words which might be used in board- or seat-work exercises include: ink, blink, drink, think; plank, drank, spank, frank; trunk, chunk, bunk.

NG   "The sound of NG at the end of words is the sound we hear in these words."

bang	king	gong	hung
gang	ring	bong	rung
hang	wing	strong	sprung
sang	sing	song	sung

CK   "The letters CK have the sound of K. Listen to the sound at the end of these words."

back	pick	dock	luck
pack	kick	lock	duck
sack	sick	block	truck
crack	trick	sock	buck

QU   Consonant digraph QU:
The letter *q* has no sound of its own and is always followed by *u,* which in this case does not function as a vowel. The combination *qu* is pronounced KW—as in quick, quack (=kwik, kwak).

Other *qu* words which might be used in teaching exercises include: queen, quart, quiet, quit, Quaker, quake, quite, quarter, quail, quarrel.

Consonant Irregularities

Fortunately, there is less variability in consonant sounds than in vowel sounds. Nevertheless, a number of consonants and consonant combinations result in pronunciation irregularities which must be taught. The majority of these would fall under one of the following headings:

    a) consonants which have more than one sound (Examples: $c = k$ or s; $g = g$ or j; $s = s$, z or zh.)

    b) consonants which are not sounded (know, light, wrap)

    c) consonant combinations with unique pronunciations (ph = f; que = k).

The letter *g* has two sounds: the hard sound of *g* as heard in the words *go, gone, game*; and the *j* sound as heard in *gem, giant, generous*. Since the hard *g* sound occurs most frequently in words used in beginning instruction, it is usually taught first. On the other hand, both sounds may be taught together if it is stressed that the hard *g* sound will be met most frequently.

The consonant *c* has two sounds. The letter *c* sounded as *k* occurs most frequently in English words (cat, cold, cut, could, came — pronounced *kat, kold, kut, kood, kām*). The consonant *c* is sounded as *s* in *city, cent, circle, center*. Eight words on the Dolch List begin with the letter *c*, and in all of these the letter has its *k* sound. Only four of the fifty-eight words on the Dale List, which begin with *c*, have the *s* sound. There is a phonic principle which applies in a number of cases:

The letter *c* has the sound of *k* (cat = *k*at), except when *c* is followed by *e*, *i*, or *y*, in which cases, *c* usually has the sound of *s*.

The following lists of words can be used for teaching the two sounds of the letter *c*. Note that in each of these words:

c is not followed by *e*, *i*, or *y* — the *c* is sounded as *k*			*c* is followed by *e*, *i*, or *y* — the *c* is sounded as *s*		
call	cat	cold	cent	city	circle
cup	cut	cake	cellar	place	center
came	coat	come	cider	cycle	voice
can	corn	cap	glance	cedar	citizen
could	carry	catch	cement	bicycle	mice
color	cow	care	certain	ceiling	cypress

Que at the end of words has the sound of *k*; usually *que* is blended with the preceding syllable.

picturesque = pĭk chûr ĕsk	plaque = plăk
antique = ăn tēk	grotesque = grō̇ tĕsk
burlesque = bûr lĕsk	clique = klēk
opaque = o pāk	brusque = brŭsk
critique = krĭ ˙tēk	technique = tĕk nēk

(Note that the final syllable in *que* words is accented.)

The letter combination *ph* has the sound of *f* (photo = foto).
Blackboard eye-ear exercise:

photograph = fō̇ tō̇ grăf	Phillip = fĭl lĭp
alphabet = ăl fá bĕt	phonograph = fŏn ȯ grăf
Philadelphia = fĭl á dĕl fĭ á	hyphen = hī̄ fĕn

Word list for teaching the sound of *ph*:

*ph*one	*ph*rase	or*ph*an	*ph*obia	saxo*ph*one
gra*ph*	ne*ph*ew	*ph*ysics	sym*ph*ony	geogra*ph*y
*ph*oto	*ph*ilosophy	as*ph*alt	em*ph*asize	*ph*onics
tele*ph*one	ty*ph*oon	pro*ph*et	*ph*ysical	pam*ph*let
autogra*ph*	*ph*ase	so*ph*omore	s*ph*ere	biogra*ph*y

The letter *s* may be sounded in several ways. The most common and the most logical sound to teach first is the *s* sound, as heard in *s*ay, *s*ell, *s*it, *s*ome, *s*unk. A single *s* sometimes has the sound of *z*: his = hiz; days = daz; as = az; runs = runz. The letter *s* is sometimes sounded *sh* as in *s*ure (= shur) and *s*ugar (= shugar), or *zh* as in *treasure*. The *sh* and *zh* sounds of *s* may be introduced much later than the *s* and *z* sounds.

Silent Consonants:

A large number of English words contain one or more silent letters. In some instances, particularly when the initial letter is silent, it pays to learn the words as sight words. Instant word recognition and independent reading are enhanced by deliberately calling to the child's attention the more frequently occurring instances of silent consonants. A number of generalizations covering silent consonants are listed below, followed by exercise material which can be used in chalk-board or seat-work exercises.

   1. In words containing double consonants, only one is sounded.
   2. In words beginning with *kn*, the *k* is usually silent.

3. The combination *gh* is usually silent when preceded by the vowel *i*.
4. In words beginning with *wr*, the *w* is usually silent.
5. In words ending with the syllable *ten*, the *t* is often silent.
6. In words containing *ck*, the *c* is usually silent.
7. In words ending with *mb*, the *b* is usually silent.

It is doubtful that learning the above rules in isolation or as a *series* of generalizations has virtue. Working with a series of stimulus words which follow one or more of these rules will help the child gain insight into the pronunciation of words. Table 2 contains words which follow one of the previously cited generalizations.

Table 2

double consonants	*kn* words	*gh* words	*-ten* ending	*-ck* ending	*-mb* ending	*wr* words
ladder	know	sigh	often	sack	comb	write
collect	knee	light	soften	neck	thumb	wring
fellow	knight	sight	listen	block	climb	wrote
message	knew	bright	hasten	kick	bomb	wrap
roller	knit	flight	fasten	duck	lamb	wrath
summer	knife	night	glisten	clock	plumb	wrist
dinner	knock	might	moisten	black	limb	wrong
yellow	kneel	slight	brighten	trick	numb	wren
happen	knob	blight	tighten	back	crumb	wreck
kitten	known	right	frighten	pick	dumb	wreath

While a given generalization may be introduced in a particular grade, it will probably have to be reviewed in subsequent grades. For some children, simple review will not be adequate. The generalization and applications will have to be retaught. By means of close observation or diagnosis, the teacher — at any grade level — discovers which children need help on a particular skill. She can work individually with these children or devise seat-work exercises which provide practice in the areas in which deficiencies are noted. Words of appropriate difficulty can be selected for use in various types of teaching exercises. The difficulty level of the exercises can be further controlled by the task or tasks which the child is called upon to perform. (See Tables 3 and 4.)

Table 3

Task I: Pronounce all the words in each *A* column.

Task II: Strike out each silent consonant in the words in the *A* columns (the first one is done for you).

Task III: In the *B* columns, write the dictionary pronunciation of each word.

A	B	A	B
sight	s̄it	knight	
hasten		glisten	
knew		comb	
rabbit		right	
thick		write	
climb		black	
wrote		funnel	
dollar		known	
debt		doubt	
knock		truck	
soften		often	
summer		tunnel	
sigh		thumb	
wrap		knelt	
knob		listen	

The following exercise illustrates that silent letters are useful in that they produce a different word which has the same pronunciation but a different meaning from the word to which the silent letter is added. The silent letter provides a VISUAL clue to the meaning of the new word.

Table 4

In Column *B*, add a silent letter or letters to each word in Column *A* in order to produce a different word.

A	B	A	B
new		rest	
hole		be	
our		cent	
rap		not	
nob		plum	
in		no	
night		to	
ring		so	

TEACHING CONTRACTIONS

Contractions are single words formed by combining two words but omitting a letter or letters. An apostrophe (') is always inserted where a letter or letters have been omitted.

Contractions result from major structural changes in words and should be taught as sight words. Two illustrative teaching and testing exercises are presented. In exercise *A*, the child selects the proper contractions from a list provided; in exercise *B*, he must *supply* the correct form from memory.

A. Write the contraction for each of the pairs of words below. The contractions you will need to use are included on the next line:

he'll, I'll, didn't, they've, haven't, isn't, mustn't, I'm

1. did not	_____	5. is not	_____
2. he will	_____	6. they have	_____
3. have not	_____	7. I will	_____
4. must not	_____	8. I am	_____

B. Write the contractions for each of the pairs of words below. Remember an apostrophe is part of the spelling.

1. is not	_____	4. should not	_____
2. I am	_____	5. they have	_____
3. they are	_____	6. you are	_____

List of contractions for use with board- or seat-work exercises:

can't, they've, I'll, it's, there's, wouldn't, doesn't, hadn't, you're, hasn't, I've, don't, she'll, shouldn't, they'd, mustn't, he'll, isn't, didn't, she's, I'm, wasn't, haven't, they're, he's, couldn't.

SUMMARY OF CONSONANT GENERALIZATIONS

1. In general, consonant letters are quite consistent in the sounds they represent. Letters which represent only one sound include *b, d, f, h, j, k, l, m, n, p, r, w*, and initial *y*.
2. Consonants which combine
    a) Consonant blends are two or more letters which are blended so that sound elements of each letter are heard — *bl*, b*l*ack; *str*, *str*ing; *spl*, *spl*ash; *gl*, *gl*ide.
    b) Consonant digraphs are two-letter combinations which result in one speech sound that is not a blend of the letters involved —*sh*all; *wh*ite; *th*is (voiced *th*); *th*ink (unvoiced *th*); *ch*air; *ch*orus (ch=k); *ch*ef (ch=sh).
3. Irregular spellings
    a) Silent consonants in specific combinations.

    1) The *k* is silent in *kn* (knew, knee).

    2) Double consonants — only one is sounded (sum~~m~~er).

    3) When vowel *i* precedes *gh*, the latter is silent (ligh~~t~~).

    4) The *w* is silent in *wr* at the beginning of words (~~w~~ring).

    5) When a word ends with the syllable *ten*, the *t* is often silent (of~~t~~en, fas~~t~~en).

    6) In *ck* combinations, *c* is silent (sa~~c~~k, clo~~c~~k).

    7) The *b* is silent in *mb* at the end of words (com~~b~~, lam~~b~~).

4. Two sounds for consonant *c*

    a) $c = k$ in *cake, corn, curl*.

    b) $c = s$ when followed by *i, e, y* (city, cent, cycle).

5. Two sounds for consonant *g*

    a) regular sound in *go, game, gum*.

    b) $g = j$ when followed by *e, i* (gem, giant).

6. *Ph* $= f$ (photo $=$ foto; graph $=$ graf).

7. *Qu* $= kw$ (quack $=$ kwack). The letter *q* has no sound of its own. In English spellings, *q* is always followed by the letter *u*.

8. The letter *s* may be sounded in a number of ways.

    a) $s = s$ (most common) (sell, soft, said).

    b) $s = z$ (his $=$ hiz; runs $=$ runz).

    c) $s = sh$, *zh* (sugar, treasure).

SUMMARY

This chapter opened with a discussion of the prerequisites a child needs in order to profit from phonics instruction. The learner must be able to:

1. make auditory discrimination between similar speech sounds

2. distinguish visually between letters.

When these abilities have not been developed, there is no basis for teaching phonic analysis. The teaching of these skills is usually stressed in what has come to be labeled the "reading-readiness program." It is essential that these important skills be seen as part of the systematic instructional program.

Once the child has acquired adequate auditory and visual discrimination skills, he is ready for instruction in associating printed letters with speech sounds. The balance of Chapter 2 provided illustrations of teaching procedures. It should be kept in mind that the intent was to present illustrative examples, rather than to prescribe. Tables 5, 6, and 7, which follow, are compilations of words which might be used in teaching particular phonic skills.

Table 5

A list of easier words for use in board- or seat-work exercises in teaching initial sound of consonants

c = k	d	f	hard g	h	j	k	l
can	did	fast	go	hat	jump	keep	let
cap	do	far	game	hand	just	kind	like
car	done	feel	gate	hill	Jane	king	love
cold	down	fall	garden	hair	Jack	kept	lady
carry	deep	first	gave	his	joy	key	light
cow	dinner	fun	gift	hold	jam	kick	look
cry	day	full	give	head	jar	kill	lake
cut	dear	father	get	hot	jelly	kiss	little
come	dark	farm	gold	have	jet	kite	last
cup	dish	face	got	he	job	kitten	listen
cat	damp	fly	gone	him	joke	Kate	letter
cake	deed	for	good	had	June	kettle	late
coat	dip	found	gain	how	join	keg	lost

m	n	p	r	s	t	v	w
most	new	pan	red	see	tell	very	walk
man	not	pass	rain	sit	ten	visit	wash
my	near	put	rest	some	to	voice	want
must	need	pull	ran	save	talk	valley	word
may	nice	paid	room	sing	took	view	wish
me	night	party	ride	say	told	velvet	work
much	noon	people	road	same	take	vote	wait
many	name	pick	run	soon	tall		window
meet	no	paper	right	sat	time		will
milk	none	paint	real	seen	too		went
made	now	pen	river	set	table		wall
meat	never	part	race	so	top		warm
mine	north	person	rat	soft	tail		win
move	next	pig	ring	said	tap		water
men	nap	pork	roll	soap	tent		winter

y		
yes	yet
you	your
yard	yellow

Table 6

A list of words for use in board- or seat-work exercises for teaching initial consonant blends

br	cr	dr	fr	gr	pr	tr
brother	cry	dress	friend	grade	pretty	tree
bring	cross	drink	from	great	present	train
brought	crop	draw	front	ground	president	trip
brown	creek	dry	Friday	green	program	truly
brake	crowd	drive	fruit	grandmother	print	trick
bread	cream	drop	fright	grass	produce	truck
bright	crack	dream	free	grandfather	prize	trade
bridge	crawl	drove	fresh	group	promise	trap
break	crib	drum	frog	grew	proud	track
brave	cried	drew	freeze	gray	product	true
brush	crumb	drill	frozen	grain	prepare	trail
branch	crown	drag	friendly	grab	protect	treat
brick	crow	drank	fry	grape	press	trim
broom	crook	drug	frost	grand	price	tramp

bl	cl	fl	pl	sl	sp	st
black	close	flower	play	sleep	spell	start
blue	clean	fly	place	sled	spend	stay
blow	class	floor	please	slid	spot	story
block	clothes	flag	plant	slate	speak	stop
bloom	climb	flew	plan	slip	spent	store
blew	club	flood	plane	slowly	sport	study
blanket	cloth	float	plenty	slave	speed	still
blood	cloud	flat	plain	slow	spoke	state
blackboard	clear	flour	plate	slipper	spirit	stand
blossom	clay		pleasant	slept	speech	stick
blind	clothing	gl	plow	sleet	spoon	stocking
blame	clock	glad	player	sleepy	spear	step
blizzard	climate	glass	plantation	slim	space	star
blaze	clown	glove	playmate	slick	spin	stood

sm	sn	sc	sk	sw	tw
small	snow	school	skate	swim	twelve
smoke	snake	scare	skin	sweet	twist
smell	snowball	scold	sky	swing	twenty
smile	snail	scout	ski	sweater	twice
smart	snap	scream	skip	swan	twin
smooth	snug	schoolhouse	skirt	sweep	twig
smack	sneeze	score	skunk	swell	twinkle

Table 7

A list of easier words for use in board- or seat-work exercises in teaching substitution of initial consonant sounds. Each series contains "family words" or words which end with a common phonogram. It will also be noted that some of these phonograms are little words—*at, an, it,* etc. However, in every case we are dealing with the *sound* that occurs at the end of a word, not with sounding little words in larger words.

back	bake	day	cap	bug	bank	cot	Dick
Jack	cake	gay	gap	dug	rank	dot	kick
lack	fake	hay	lap	hug	sank	got	lick
pack	lake	lay	map	jug	tank	hot	nick
rack	make	may	nap	mug	(blank)	lot	pick
sack	rake	pay	rap	rug	(crank)	not	sick
tack	sake	ray	tap	tug	(drank)	pot	(brick)
(black)	take	say	(clap)	(chug)	(flank)	(blot)	(chick)
(crack)	wake	way	(flap)	(drug)	(frank)	(plot)	(click)
(shack)	(brake)	(clay)	(slap)	(plug)	(plank)	(shot)	(slick)
(slack)	(flake)	(play)	(snap)	(slug)	(prank)	(slot)	(stick)
(stack)	(shake)	(stray)	(strap)	(smug)	(spank)	(spot)	(thick)
(track)	(snake)	(tray)	(trap)	(snug)	(thank)	(trot)	(trick)

bag	bail	gain	bat	bump	can	came	Bill
gag	fail	lain	cat	dump	Dan	dame	fill
lag	hail	main	fat	hump	fan	fame	hill
nag	mail	pain	hat	jump	man	game	kill
rag	nail	rain	mat	lump	pan	lame	mill
sag	pail	vain	pat	pump	ran	name	pill
tag	rail	(brain)	rat	(chump)	tan	same	will
wag	sail	(drain)	sat	(plump)	van	tame	(drill)
(brag)	tail	(grain)	(brat)	(slump)	(bran)	(blame)	(skill)
(drag)	(frail)	(plain)	(flat)	(stump)	(clan)	(flame)	(spill)
(flag)	(trail)	(train)	(scat)	(thump)	(plan)	(frame)	(still)
(snag)	(snail)						

best	bet	bunk	bell	bit	dim	dear	bad
lest	get	dunk	fell	fit	him	fear	dad
nest	jet	hunk	sell	hit	Jim	hear	fad
pest	let	junk	tell	pit	rim	near	had
rest	met	sunk	well	sit	Tim	rear	lad
test	net	(drunk)	yell	wit	(brim)	tear	mad
vest	pet	(flunk)	(shell)	(flit)	(grim)	year	pad
zest	set	(skunk)	(smell)	(grit)	(slim)	(clear)	sad
(blest)	wet	(spunk)	(spell)	(slit)	(swim)	(smear)	(glad)
(crest)	(fret)	(trunk)	(swell)	(split)	(trim)	(spear)	

Table 7 (Cont.)

bold	hop	bed	buck	band	beat	bend	ball	bun
cold	mop	fed	duck	hand	heat	lend	call	fun
fold	pop	led	luck	land	meat	mend	fall	gun
gold	top	Ned	suck	sand	neat	send	hall	run
hold	(crop)	red	tuck	(brand)	seat	tend	tall	sun
mold	(drop)	Ted	(pluck)	(gland)	(cheat)	(blend)	wall	(spun)
sold	(flop)	(bled)	(struck)	(grand)	(treat)	(spend)	(small)	(stun)
told	(shop)	(fled)	(stuck)	(stand)	(wheat)		(stall)	
(scold)	(stop)	(sled)	(truck)					

Chapter 3

Teaching Vowel Sounds

Teaching vowel sounds is undoubtedly the most difficult part of phonics instruction. This is true primarily because of the great variability in sound that a vowel or vowel combination may represent in different words. Some of these differences are quite minute, and being unable to distinguish between them would not seriously handicap a person in learning to read—assuming, of course, that he can pronounce the words in question. For instance, the differences in the sound of the vowel *a* in *loyal, almost, idea, path, father* are not likely to pose a problem in beginning reading. To profit from phonics instruction, one must be able to discriminate between such vowel sounds as are heard in the words *pin, pen, pan, pun; apple, able; book, boot; not, note;* and the like.

In teaching phonic analysis, deciding which vowel, or which sound of that vowel to teach first, is probably not a crucial issue. The reasons usually advanced for teaching the short sounds first are these:

1. A majority of the words a child meets in beginning reading contain short vowel sounds.

2. Many of these words are single-vowel-in-medial-position words. The phonic generalization covering this situation holds or applies in a large percentage of words met in beginning reading: One vowel in the middle of a word (or syllable) usually has its short sound.

Advocacy of teaching long vowel sounds first rests on the fact that the vowel name *is* the long sound of the vowel (A E I O U). It is frequently suggested that this fact makes it easy to teach the letter-sound association. It should be recalled that one of the virtues of teaching some sight-recognition words either before or concurrently with phonic analysis is that the sight words learned can then serve as "phonic models." In this approach children work with sounds as heard in words, not sounds assigned to letters in isolation. This latter practice was one of the major weaknesses of earlier phonics instruction. Children worked with sounds of letters divorced from how the letters sounded in KNOWN words:

C was pronounced *kuh*; *A = ah*; *T = tuh*; *kuh at tuh = cat*.

As one begins the teaching of vowel sounds, it is important to keep in mind what learnings have taken place prior to this activity:

1. The child understands and uses spoken language.

2. The school has provided extended practice on auditory-visual discrimination.

3. Children have likely learned a number of SIGHT words.

4. Sounds of consonants have been learned:

   m sounds as heard in *man, milk, mop*

   c sounds as heard in *cat (kat), cake*

   t sounds as heard in *take, toy*—and other consonant sounds.

TEACHING SHORT *A* SOUND

There are two approaches to teaching the short sound of vowels in words of one syllable. One of these is to deal separately with single initial and medial vowels. The other combines the teaching of these two vowel situations. The generalizations on which either approach is based are:

1. A single vowel in medial position usually has its short sound.

2. A single vowel which does not conclude a word usually has its short sound.

In the material which follows, the short sounds of the vowels in medial position are taught first, followed by an illustration of teaching single initial and single medial vowels together.

The teacher may say, "We have learned the sounds that consonants stand for in words. You can hear the sound of *b* in *bat*, *d* in *dad*, *m* in man.[1] Now we are going to learn to hear the sounds that vowels stand for in words. The vowel letters are A a, E e, I i, O o, U u." (Pronounce each letter as it is written on the chalkboard. Then point to the various letters and invite the children to name them.) "When we

---

[1] The concept being taught is that printed letters *represent* speech sounds. However, in working with children, teachers will likely use other terms.

say the name of the vowel letter, we hear what is called the vowel's long sound.

"Today we are going to listen carefully and learn to hear another sound for the vowel *a*—its short sound. I am going to put some words on the board. We have studied these words before. Each of the words has the letter *a* in it. Listen to the sound the *a* has in each word."

```
cat
stand
man
ham
cap
back
```

1. Pronounce each word, moving hand from left to right through the word.

2. Emphasize the sound of *a* (*ah*), but do not distort the sound.

3. Have the children say the words in unison, asking them to listen for the sound of ă.

4. Stress that the sound heard is called the short sound of *a*. Have the children note how this sound differs from the letter name.

5. Ask pupils how many vowels they see in each word and where the vowel is located (middle of word).

6. Have children state what sound is heard when there is one vowel in the middle of a word.[2]

7. Have children state, in their own words, the rule which covers this vowel situation.[3]

Using this approach the generalization will evolve: One vowel in the middle of the word usually has its short sound. It is probably not essential that each child be able to recite all of the generalizations discussed in this chapter. At this point, it might be profitable to cite other familiar words which follow the generalizations under discussion, even though all the stimulus words used are not yet known as sight words.

---

[2] Strictly speaking, the vowel in words such as *back, bank, trap*, are not in the middle of the word. Children are usually not confused by this statement, but a teacher can modify the generalization if she wishes.

[3] From the standpoint of the teacher, the generalizations which apply to vowel situations do not qualify as rules. However, in teaching children, these generalizations are called rules and each is qualified by the term "usually."

A	B
ran	răn
bat	băt
Sam	Săm
bag	băg
bank	bănk
trap	trăp
glad	glăd
hat	hăt

1. Place on the board other words, all of which have the single vowel *a* in medial position.

2. Have children note short sound of *a*. (If the teacher wishes, she may mark the vowels ă, explaining this mark [˘] may be used to indicate the short vowel sound. See Column *B*.)

Below are a number of words which have the medial short *a* sound. These are usually met in beginning or early primary level reading.

bad	camp	fact	hat	match	stand
back	cat	flag	hang	plan	shall
bat	clap	flat	Jack	pal	sack
band	catch	flash	lamp	pan	sank
bang	dad	grand	land	pat	sang
bank	dash	grab	lad	quack	tan
black	drag	hand	man	rag	track
cap	fan	had	map	ranch	thank
can	fat	ham	mad	sad	

SHORT SOUND OF *I*

Review

1. "Who can name the vowels?"
2. "What vowel did we study last?"
3. "Today we will listen for the short sound of the vowel *i*. Remember, the short sound of vowels is marked ˘. I am going to put some

words on the board—words we have already studied. All the words will have the vowel *i* in them. Listen and hear how the *i* is sounded when we pronounce the words."

Steps

1. Teacher pronounces each word.
2. Children (in unison) pronounce each word.

3. Children note:
   a) Each word contains the vowel *i*.
   b) The vowel is in the middle of the word.
   c) *I* has its short sound.
4. Call for rule previously learned: One vowel in the middle of a word (usually) has the short sound.
5. Have children volunteer other words with medial short *i* to be listed on board.

Variation: Use of Word Families

Some teachers find that certain children can do better in "fixing" the short sound of a given vowel if they see and pronounce a series of words which contain larger identical units than the vowel alone: the words *big, ship, tin, hill* have an identical unit—*i*. The words *big, pig, dig, fig*; or *hill, fill, bill, pill*; or *sit, fit, bit, kit* have rhyming units composed of several letters which have precisely the same phonic value in each word. Word families could be used both for teaching common phonic elements and for rapid recognition as sight words.

Below are a number of words containing the medial short *i* sound. These words are usually met in beginning or early primary-level reading.

tin	sit	did	will	ring	pick	big
fin	bit	lid	hill	king	kick	dig
win	fit	hid	still	sing	sick	fig
pin	hit	rid	mill	bring	stick	pig
skin	kit	bid	Bill	spring	thick	wig

TEACHING THE SHORT SOUND OF *E*

1. Review concepts previously introduced.
   a) Have pupils name the vowels.
   b) Tell what vowel sounds have been studied previously.
   c) State the rule learned: One vowel in the middle of a word usually has its short sound.
2. Put short *e* stimulus words on board. (Column *A* illustrates word-family endings, Column *B* — mixed endings.)

A	B
bet	pen
get	dress
pet	let
let	bell
set	red

3. Teacher pronounces words.
4. Pupils say words, listening to sound of *e*.
5. Invite restatement of generalization "one vowel in medial position . . . ."
6. Have children suggest other words.
7. Reinforce learning with seat-work exercises. Make sure child does not rely on *visual cues* alone.
8. Teacher works with small groups or with individual children who have not mastered concepts and letter-sound relationships taught thus far.

Words containing short *e* sound (medial position) which can be used in board work or in preparing seat-work exercises:

tell	ten	pet	led	help	dress	yes
sell	men	let	red	held	less	west
well	pen	met	fed	rest	sled	send
fell	hen	set	bed	step	kept	tent
smell	den	yet	Ted	sent	spell	best

SHORT SOUND OF *U*

Follow steps outlined previously for teaching short vowel sounds.
1. Put short *u* stimulus words on board.

2. Column *A* illustrates word-family endings; Column *B* — mixed endings.

A	B
bug	bus
hug	tub
dug	pup
rug	jump
jug	much

3. Teacher pronounces words, then pupils say words listening for the sound of *u*.

4. Review rule learned previously.

5. Reinforce learning with seat-work exercises. Make sure child does not rely on visual cues alone.

6. Teacher works with small groups or with individual children who have not mastered sounds and concepts taught thus far.

7. Review words having short *a*, *i*, or *e* sound.

Words containing short *u* sound (medial position) which can be used in board work or in preparing seat-work exercises:

gun	rub	bump	duck	sunk	jug
run	tub	dump	luck	chum	rug
fun	club	jump	truck	fuss	dug
sun	must	gum	suck	dull	bug
bun	trust	hum	hung	but	drum
cup	bust	sum	sung	cut	bud
shut	dust	puff	rung	hut	stub

SHORT SOUND OF *O*

Follow steps outlined previously in teaching short vowel sounds (a, i, e, u, above).

1. "Who will name the vowels?"

2. "What vowel sounds have we studied?"

3. "Who can say the rule we have learned?" One vowel in middle of word or syllable usually has its short sound.

4. Put short *o* stimulus words on board.

5. Column *A* contains word-family endings, Column *B* — mixed endings.

```
┌─────────────────────────┐
│    A          B          │
│   got        shot        │
│   hot        rock        │
│   lot        doll        │
│   not        box         │
│   pot        drop        │
└─────────────────────────┘
```

6. Pupils pronounce words, listening to the sound of *o*.

7. Invite pupils to supply other words which contain short *o* sound in medial position.

8. Reinforce learning with seat-work exercises.

Words containing short *o* sound (medial position) which can be used in board work or in preparing seat-work exercises:

hop	got	pond	job	fox	block
stop	hot	frog	rob	clock	shot
drop	not	sock	Bob	nod	log
pop	pot	shop	sob	lock	box
mop	cot	rock	cob	trot	top

TEACHING SHORT SOUND OF INITIAL AND MEDIAL VOWELS AS ONE GENERALIZATION

Some teachers prefer to teach the short sound of *initial* and *medial* vowels simultaneously. The procedure can be much the same as discussed above for the medial-vowel situation. However, the generalization which emerges will be stated differently. To illustrate this concept, place a number of stimulus words on the board.

```
┌──────────┐  ┌──────────┐
│    A      │  │    B      │
│   act     │  │   hat     │
│   am      │  │   ran     │
│   as      │  │   shall   │
│   at      │  │   hand    │
│   ask     │  │   man     │
└──────────┘  └──────────┘
```

Words in Column *A* contain one vowel (initial), and the short sound is heard. Words in Column *B* contain one vowel (medial), and the short vowel is heard. As the children see and hear these characteristics, the following generalization will emerge:

When there is one vowel in a word and the vowel does not come at the end of the word, it has its short sound.

THE SCHWA SOUND

In a large number of words of more than one syllable, there is a diminished stress on one of the syllables. The sound of the vowel in these unstressed syllables undergoes a slight change which is referred to as "a softening of the vowel sound." This softened vowel sound is called the *schwa* sound, and is represented by the symbol ə.

All of the vowels are represented by the schwa sound as illustrated by each of the italicized vowels in the following words.

$$
\begin{aligned}
\text{bedl}a\text{m} &= \text{bed}'\ \text{ləm} \\
\text{beat}en &= \text{b}\bar{\text{e}}\text{t}'\ \text{ən} \\
\text{beaut}ifu\text{l} &= \text{b}\bar{\text{u}}'\ \text{tə}\ \text{fəl} \\
\text{beck}on &= \text{bek}'\ \text{ən}
\end{aligned}
$$

In other words, if vowels were interchanged in unstressed syllables, the spellings would change but the sound heard would remain the same for the different vowels. For instance, read both of the following sentences without stressing the second syllable in any word.

A. "Button, button, who has the button?"
B. "Buttun, buttan, who has the butten?"

If, in reading sentence *B* you give each second syllable the same stress as it was given in the word directly above it, the sounds remain constant. Thus, teaching the schwa sound in the initial stages of reading would have little impact on one's ability to sound out words. However, once the child begins to use a dictionary which utilizes the schwa symbol, ə, the points discussed above would have to be explained.

Teaching the Generalization Involving Two Adjacent Vowels

When two vowels are together, the first usually has its long sound and the second is silent. In the illustrations which follow, teaching does not start with a statement of the generalization, but with material which will help children discover the generalization. The two-vowel generalization holds fairly consistently for *ee, oa, ai, ea,* and does not apply equally well for *au, ou, ui, eu.*

Table 8

Percent of instances in which the two-vowel rule applies[4]

ee	oa	ai	ea	"final e"	ui	all two-vowel situations combined
98%	97%	64%	66%	63%	6%	45%

One way to illustrate and teach this generalization is to place four columns of words on the board. Each column should consist of words which contain one of the vowel combinations *oa, ai, ea,* or *ee.*

1	2	3	4
boat	chain	beat	feed
coat	mail	dream	seed
load	wait	leaf	keep
road	rain	teach	queen
soak	paid	seat	steel

1. Pronounce each word in the first column, emphasizing the long $\bar{o}$ sound.

2. Repeat for each column, emphasizing vowel sound heard.

3. Have child note visual pattern of two vowels. Point out that in each word, you *hear* the long sound of the first vowel and that the second vowel is not sounded.

$$\text{boat} = \text{b } \bar{o} \not{a} \text{ t} = \text{b}\bar{o}\text{t} \qquad \text{beat} = \text{b } \bar{e} \not{a} \text{ t} = \text{b}\bar{e}\text{t}$$
$$\text{rain} = \text{r } \bar{a} \not{i} \text{ n} = \text{r}\bar{a}\text{n} \qquad \text{feed} = \text{f } \bar{e} \not{e} \text{ d} = \text{f}\bar{e}\text{d}$$

A second illustration is to place a column of single-medial vowels on the board (Column *A*). Have children note that they hear the short vowel sound. Then, write words in Column *B*, leaving a vacant letter space following each vowel. Add second vowel as found in words in Column *C*. In each case, a different word is built in which the first vowel has its long sound and the second is silent. Other word combinations include: met—meet—meat; lad—laid; mad—maid; plan—plain; bed—bead; net—neat; step—steep.

---

[4] Theodore Clymer, "The Utility of Phonic Generalizations In The Primary Grades," *The Reading Teacher,* XVI, January, 1963, pp. 252–58. Also see bibliography following Chapter 1.

A	B	C
set	se t	seat
cot	co t	coat
men	me n	mean
fed	fe d	feed
got	go t	goat
pan	pa n	pain
man	ma n	main
bet	be t	beat

Below are a number of *oa, ai, ea,* and *ee* words which may be used in board-work or seat-work exercises.

oa		*ai*		*ea*		*ee*	
boat	roam	rain	maid	eat	reach	deep	week
goat	coach	mail	grain	bead	clean	street	feel
soap	boast	gain	laid	bean	cream	meet	queen
coat	goal	sail	trail	deal	meal	feed	wheel
coal	coast	pain	plain	clean	meat	keep	speed
roast	groan	fail	train	steal	speak	seen	feed
float	foam	paid	tail	leak	mean	sleep	sheep
soak	toast	nail	chain	beach	dream	need	green

Teaching the Generalization Involving Final e

In two-vowel words the final *e* is silent and the previous vowel usually has its long sound.

1. Place a column of words on the board which have a single vowel in medial position. Choose words to which a final *e* may be added to form a new word and illustrate this generalization (see Column *A*).

2. Pupils pronounce words in Column *A*.

3. Cite previously learned rule (single vowel in medial position usually has short sound).

4. Add final *e* to each word (as in Column *B*).

5. Pupils pronounce words in Column *B* and listen to vowel sound heard.

6. Ask children for generalization (the final *e* is silent and the first vowel is long).

7. If desired, diacritical marks may be used in Column *C*.

A	B	C
hat	hate	h ā t ̸e
hid	hide	h ī d ̸e
past	paste	p ā s t ̸e
pal	pale	p ā l ̸e
cut	cute	c ū t ̸e
plan	plane	p l ā n ̸e
rat	rate	r ā t ̸e
pin	pine	p ī n ̸e
strip	stripe	s t r ī p ̸e
ride	ride	r ī d ̸e

Other words which can be used in board-work or seat-work lessons include: fat, bath, rip, tap, twin, mat, quit, fin, win, cap, bit, dim, can, kit, pan, etc.

Exceptions to Rule: Since a number of frequently met words, particularly o + e words, do not follow the rule, some teachers prefer to deal with this fact rather than ignore it. Teachers might point out several exceptions, noting that applying the above rule will not help in solving the words.

love	done	none	come	have	lĭve
dove	gone	glove	some	give	sense

Teaching Generalization of Single-Final Vowel

When the only vowel in a word comes at the end of the word, it has its long sound. In general, this statement also applies to single vowels which conclude accented syllables.

1. Place words on the board that contain one vowel in final position.

2. Review fact that *y* at the end of a word functions as a vowel (*y* = long *i*).

3. Teacher and pupils pronounce each word.

4. "What do you SEE that is the same in each of these words?" (They all end with one vowel.)

5. "What do you HEAR in each of these words?" (The long vowel sound.)

6. "Could we make up a rule to fit all of these words?" (Children will say the rule in their own words and the teacher restates and writes rule on the board.)

he	go	by	try
she	no	my	fly
we	so	cry	sky
me		dry	why
be		fry	shy

Teaching the Generalization Covering ay

Ay at the end of words has the sound of long *a*.

1. Children have learned: The vowels are *a–e–i–o–u* and sometimes *y*. When *y* functions as a vowel it:
   - *a*) concludes a word which has no other vowel
   - *b*) concludes words of more than one syllable (happy)
   - *c*) immediately follows another vowel.
2. In the combination *ay*, *y* serves as a vowel. Two vowels together — the second is silent, the first has its long sound.
3. Place stimulus words on board.

```
day
may
stay
say
clay
```

4. Teacher and pupils pronounce words.
5. Vowel sound heard — long sound of *a*.

Other illustrations: gay, lay, hay, play, stray, pay, ray, jay, may, fay, sway, spray, away, pray, tray, gray.

Sound of y at End of Longer Words

When *y* concludes a word of two or more syllables, it has the sound heard in: hob *by*, win *dy*, fog *gy*, luc *ky*, jol *ly*, fun *ny*, hap *py*, mer *ry*, noi *sy*, rus *ty*, buz *zy*.

Most dictionaries mark this sound of *y* as short *i* (ĭ—hur ĭ, luck ĭ, etc.). However, many authorities feel that the final sound heard in the above words is closer to long *e* (ē).[5] The writer agrees with the latter position, but each teacher will have to decide this issue for herself.

Other words which might be used in teaching exercises: badly, angry, plenty, cooky, honestly, closely, beauty, mainly, guilty, history, lively, nasty, January, partly, ready, seventy, rocky, penny, muddy, simply, sorry, jelly, nearly, costly, sleepy.

TEACHING LONG AND SHORT SOUNDS TOGETHER

The sequence in which vowel sounds are taught is probably not crucial. The rationale for teaching long sounds first and that for teaching short sounds first has been reviewed previously. (See p. 53.) Some teachers prefer to present both long and short sounds together in order to help the child hear the difference. Immediately following this approach, one or the other sound may be worked with extensively.

The following procedure might be used for contrasting the long and short sounds of the same vowel. The illustration will deal with only one vowel—*a*.

1. "Today we want to see if we can hear the difference between two sounds that the vowel *A* stands for."

A - a	
I	**II**
rain	ran
main	man
paid	pad
maid	mad
pail	pal
pain	pan

2. Place upper- and lower-case letter on board.
3. Place long-vowel words on board (Column I).
4. Pronounce each word for children.
   a) "Do you hear the sound *a*?"

---

[5] See Leonard Bloomfield and Clarence L. Barnhart, *Let's Read* (Detroit: Wayne State University Press, 1961), p. 210; and Dolores Durkin, *Phonics and the Teaching of Reading* (No. 22, Bureau of Publications, Teachers College, Columbia University [New York, 1962]), p. 63.

    b) "Do you hear the letter's name?"

    c) "When you hear the letter's name, that is its long sound—*a*."

5. Have the pupils note:

    a) Each of these words has two vowels.

    b) The first "says its name" (i.e., long sound).

    c) The second is silent.

6. Next add the words in Column II.

    a) Pronounce each word.

    b) Contrast vowel sounds heard in *rain, ran,* etc.

7. Have pupils note:

    a) Each of these words has one vowel.

    b) The vowel is in the middle of the word.

    c) The short sound of the vowel is heard.

EXAMPLES OF EXERCISES FOR TEACHING VOWEL SOUNDS

A. Do you have a "good ear" for vowel sounds? In this exercise each vowel you see is one of the following:

    1. not sounded (Use this mark / ; seed.)

    2. short (Use this mark ˘ ; it.)

    3. long (Use this mark ⁻ ; seed.)

Say each word—listen to the sound you hear. Then mark each vowel using one of the above marks. (The diacritical marks are included for the teacher's ease in scoring.)

a	*e*	*i*	*o*	*u*
1. bănd	creăm	piȩ	clŏck	cutȩ
2. palȩ	spĕll	hĭll	gō	bŭnch
3. graȉn	kēȩp	bītȩ	cōȧl	dŭll
4. thănk	drĕss	shĭp	flōȧt	fūsȩ
5. maȉl	bēȧch	twīnȩ	shŏt	trŭck
6. rātȩ	strēȩt	skĭn	stōlȩ	mŭst

B. The above exercise can be made more difficult by omitting the vowel heading for each column and mixing vowel sounds within columns.

EXCEPTIONS TO VOWEL RULES PREVIOUSLY TAUGHT

There is no vowel rule or generalization which will apply in all situations. When exceptions to a given rule occur, they may be taught as sight words or a new rule can be devised to cover the exception. It has been suggested that children not be burdened with rules that have very limited applications. Different teachers will, of course, arrive at different conclusions as to which generalizations should be included in phonic instruction. Some exceptions to a given rule occur with such frequency as to merit calling the child's attention to the exceptions.

For instance, one of the most useful phonic generalizations discussed earlier states: "One vowel in medial position usually has its short sound." There follow several series of words which meet the criterion of "one vowel in medial position" but in which the vowel has its long sound.

The vowel o *followed by* ld *usually has the long sound*			*The vowel* i *followed by* nd, gh, *or* ld *frequently has the long sound*		
old	hold	sold	find	light	wild
mold	told	cold	blind	fight	mild
gold	fold	bold	behind	sight	child
			mind	right	
			kind		

VOWEL SOUNDS AFFECTED BY *R*

A vowel (or vowels) followed by the letter *r* results in a blended sound which is neither the short nor long sound of the vowel.

It is doubtful that this phonic fact—as it relates to learning to read—is of paramount importance. However, calling the child's attention to this role of the letter *r* is a justifiable procedure. Since the child uses and understands hundreds of words which include a vowel followed by *r*, this is not a particularly difficult fact to teach. More important, the child will have mastered several such words as sight words, and these can serve as examples when the generalization is introduced.

Some of the more common "vowel -*r*" words which may be used in board-work or seat-work exercises are listed below.

-*ar*		-*er*	-*or*
car	yard	her	for
farm	park	person	corn
march	card	term	storm
part	far	serve	horn
star	smart	ever	short
dark	arm	certain	north
hard	bark	berth	horse
barn	tar	herd	corner
start	spark	under	form

The spelling *ir* is usually pronounced *ûr* (bird = bûrd), except when followed by a final *e* (fire):

bird	dirt	firm	third	fir	thirst
girl	first	sir	shirt	birth	stir

A FOLLOWED BY *L*, *LL*, *W*, AND *U*

The letter *a* has the sound *ô* (*aw*) when it is followed by l, ll, w, u:

talk	all	wall	saw	claw	haul
walk	tall	fall	draw	straw	because
salt	small	call	lawn	drawn	fault
halt	hall	ball	drawn	jaw	Paul

THE *oo* SOUNDS

Explaining the sounds of *oo* is much more complicated than actually learning to arrive at the correct pronunciation of the frequently used words which contain this letter combination. Most words containing *oo* are pronounced in one of two ways. These sounds are designated *ōo* (long sound) and *ŏo* (short sound). In order to be meaningful, they must be associated with something the child knows. His speaking and listening vocabulary includes some words which have the short sound and some which have the long sound. The child needs practice in hearing the differences in these sounds.

This may be accomplished by pronouncing and discriminating between these sounds in known words.

"The boot is larger than the foot."
"The moose drank from the cool pool."
"He took a look at the brook."

In the final analysis, it is the context that helps the child arrive at the correct pronunciation. For convenience in building board- or seatwork exercises, a number of *ōo* and *ŏo* words are listed below:

ōo				*ŏo*	
boo	soon	moon	boost	book	foot
cool	tool	broom	loop	good	took
food	boot	pool	hoot	stood	look
room	boon	loose	moose	shook	crook
tooth	zoo	root	proof	wood	hook

There are a few *oo* words which are neither *ōo* or *ŏo*, such as:

blood = blŭd;   flood = flŭd
door = dōr;   floor = flōr

These should be taught as sight words.

DIPHTHONGS

Diphthongs are two adjacent vowels, each of which contributes to the sound heard. The diphthongs discussed here are *ou, ow, oi, oy*. In pronouncing diphthongs, the two vowel sounds are blended as in:

h*ou*se *ow*l *oi*l b*oy*

1. The diphthongs *oi* and *oy* have the same sound (boy = b*oi*; boil = b*oil*).
2. The diphthongs *ou* and *ow* have the same sound (plow = pl*ou*; now = n*ou*).
3. The above vowel combinations are diphthongs only when pronounced as in h*ou*se, *ow*l, *oi*l, b*oy*.

Teaching Diphthong Sounds

1. Place several words on the board, all of which illustrate the diphthong sound *oi* (Column A).

A	B
oil	boy
join	toys
noise	joy
point	Roy

2. Pronounce each word for pupils.
3. Have pupils note that these words do not follow the rule: Two vowels together—the first has its long sound, and the second is silent.
4. Point out that each vowel contributes to the sound heard.

A	B
out	down
house	plow
cloud	now
round	clown

5. Place on the board words containing the diphthong *oy* (see Column *B*).

6. Point out that *oi* and *oy* represent the same sound.

7. Place on board stimulus words containing *ou* and *ow*. Pronounce each word.

8. Follow steps outlined in items 2, 3, and 4 above, pointing out that *ou* and *ow* represent the same sounds.

List of diphthong words which might be used in board- or seat-work drill:

cow	owl	mouse	mouth	boil	boy
how	gown	sound	proud	coin	toy
brown	howl	loud	shout	toil	oyster
tower	brow	couch	found	joint	joy
crown	town	south	count	soil	Troy
powder	fowl	ground	bound	moist	

Teaching ow as Long Sound of o

In a number of English words the *ow* combination has the sound of long $\bar{o}$, and may be taught as follows.

1. The letter combination *ow* has two sounds: the diphthong sound heard in "pl*ow*" and the $\bar{o}$ heard in "sn*ow*."

A	B
cow	low
plow	snow
how	grow
owl	show
town	howl

2. Pronounce the words in Column *A* — pupils listening to the sound of *ow*.

3. Pronounce pairs of words: *cow, low*; pupils listening to contrasting sounds.

4. Pupils pronounce words.

5. Point out that as words are read in context, the proper sound becomes obvious since the children know these words.

HOMONYMS

Homonyms are words that have the same pronunciation but different spellings and meanings. These words involve both structural- and phonic-analysis skills. Some homonyms follow one of the generalizations introduced previously. Many do not. For example, the rule "two vowels together — the first is long, and the second is silent" applies to both words in the following pairs:

meet — meat; see — sea; week — weak

In some instances the above rule applies to one word in a pair, the final -e rule to the other word:

road — rode; sail — sale; pain — pane

Some pairs involve silent consonants:

rap — wrap; new — knew; our — hour

Other examples of phonic irregularities:

wait — weight; wood — would; ate — eight; piece — peace

Other homonyms which might be used in board- or seat-work exercises:

beat — beet	maid — made	pair — pare
know — no	so — sew	mail — male
hear — here	hair — hare	steel — steal
there — their	by — buy	waist — waste
sun — son	fair — fare	one — won
whole — hole	dear — deer	some — sum
oh — owe	not — knot	tail — tale

SUMMARY

There is considerable variability in the sound of vowels and vowel combinations in English. This increases the difficulty of teaching or learning vowel sounds. The sequence in which vowel sounds are taught —that is, whether to teach long or short sounds first, or which vowels to teach first—is probably not an issue of great significance. A number of procedures for teaching are included above. These are meant to be illustrative rather than prescriptive. A number of generalizations covering vowel situations are also discussed. These include the following:

1. A single vowel in medial position in a word or syllable usually has its short sound (man, bed, fit).

EXCEPTIONS:

    a) The vowel *o* followed by *ld* usually has its long sound: sōld — cōld; ōld — gōld.

    b) The vowel *i* followed by *nd, gh, ld* often has its long sound: fīnd — līght — chīld.

    c) The vowel *a* = *aw* when it is followed by *l, ll, w, u*: walk, fall, draw, because.

    d) A vowel followed by the letter *r* results in a blended sound which is neither the short nor long sound of the vowel: *car, her, for.*

    e) The spelling *ir* is usually pronounced *ur* (bird = burd) except when followed by a final *e* (fire).

These exceptions are usually treated as separate generalizations.

2. When there are two vowels together, the first usually represents its long sound, and the second is silent. (This generalization applies most frequently to *ee, oa, ea, ai*: fēₑd, bōₐt, bēₐt, māịl.)

3. In words with two vowels, one of which is final *e*, the *e* is usually silent and the first vowel is usually long. (tākₑ, tūbₑ)

4. *Ay* at the end of a word has the long sound of *a*. (may, pay, play)

5. When the only vowel in a word (or accented syllable) comes at the end of the word (or syllable), it usually has its long sound.

6. When *y* concludes a word of two or more syllables, it has the sound heard in *lucky, badly.* (Sometimes taught as short *i*; *luck i*; sometimes as long *e*.)

Y functions as a vowel when it

    a) concludes a word which has no other vowel

    b) concludes words of more than one syllable (happy)

    c) follows another vowel (may).

7. Diphthongs are two adjacent vowels, each of which contributes to the sound heard (h*ou*se, pl*ow*, *oi*l, b*oy*).

8. The combination *ow* is sometimes pronounced as long ō. (Snow, show — context provides major clue to pronunciation.)

SIGHT-WORD LIST AND INFORMAL PHONICS TEST

Table 9 is a list of words, most of which are met in primary reading, which illustrate irregular spellings. From the standpoint of spoken language, all words are phonetic. However, the spellings of these words (visual patterns) are such that the more common phonic generalizations learned in beginning reading will not apply.

Table 10 is an informal test of phonic skills consisting of seven brief subtests.

Table 9: Sight-Word List

(Words with irregular spellings — confusion between
letters seen and sounds heard)

above	could	ghost	love	quiet	together
across	couple	give			ton
again	cousin	gives	machine	ranger	tongue
against	cruel	gloves	many	ready	too
aisle	curve	gone	measure	really	touch
already		great	might	right	two
another	dead	guard	mild	rough	
answer	deaf	guess	million		use
anxious	debt	guest	mind	said	usual
any	desire	guide	minute	says	
	do		mischief	school	vein
bear	does	have	mother	science	very
beautiful	done	head	move	scissors	view
beauty	don't	heart	Mr.	sew	
because	double	heaven	Mrs.	shoe	was
been	doubt	heavy		should	wash
behind	dove	here	neighbor	sign	weather
believe	dozen	high	neither	snow	weight
bind			night	soften	were
both	early	idea	none	soldier	what
bough	earn	Indian		some	where
bread	eight	instead	ocean	someone	who
break	enough	isle	of	something	whom
bright	eye		office	sometime	whose
brought	eyes	key	often	son	wild
build		kind	oh	soul	wind
built	father	knee	once	special	wolf
bury	fence	knew	one	spread	woman
busy	field	knife	onion	square	women
buy	fight	know	only	steak	won
	find		other	straight	would
calf	folks	language	ought	sure	wrong
captain	four	laugh		sword	
caught	freight	laughed	patient		you
chief	friend	leather	piece	their	young
child	front	library	pretty	there	your
clothes		light	pull	they	
colt	garage	lion	purpose	though	
coming	get	live	push	thought	
cough	getting	lived	put	to	

Table 10: Phonics-Skills Test

Subtest A (pronunciation)

(Initial and final consonant sounds; short vowel sounds)

dad	self	but	ten	lift
fuss	yell	hog	sand	muff
lamp	him	jug	get	nap
puff	web	miss	pond	kill
rag	gum	pill	rob	cob
van	top	big	held	fond

Subtest B (pronunciation)

(Initial consonant blends; long and short vowel sounds)

bring	split	blue	smoke	scream
throat	clay	club	string	trip
please	twist	float	trade	glass
sky	prize	grass	flag	snail
crop	drill	blow	scene	sweet
spray	free	sled	spoon	stay

Subtest C (pronunciation)

(Consonant digraphs [ch, sh, th, wh, qu, ng, ck]; consonant blends)

quite	thank	check	shrink	crash
church	block	length	queen	shake
shake	quick	shove	choose	think
splash	strong	thing	truck	deck
whale	chose	which	sprung	hung
fresh	wheat	quench	tenth	quack

Subtest D (pronunciation)

(Compound words; inflectional endings; contractions)

keeping	something	it's	bakery	really
pleased	can't	everybody	likes	finding
stops	quickly	lived	someone	helped
I'll	into	calls	he'll	outside
anyone	tallest	you'll	prettiest	loudest
unlock	happily	going	everything	wasn't

Table 10 (Cont.)

Subtest E (syllabication)

(In the blank spaces, write the word in separate syllables.)

candy	_can dy_	detective	_____
moment	_____	situation	_____
locomotive	_____	tiger	_____
formation	_____	education	_____
summer	_____	slippery	_____
tumble	_____	release	_____

Subtest F (prefixes, suffixes, and syllabication)

(Pronounce each word; divide each word into syllables [see example].)

dis/con/tent/ment	prehistorical	disloyalty
recaptured	disgraceful	indebtedness
incapable	imperfection	previewing
unhappily	expandable	readjustment
exporter	independently	impassable
removable	rearrangement	submerged

Subtest G

(Sustained-reading passage)

Fred and Frank planned to go on a trip to the pond. Frank liked to swim, but Fred was not a swimmer. He chose to hunt frogs and trap crabs. With a shout, the boys were off on their hike to the lake. At first, they tried to walk in the shade. Then both took off their shirts to get a sun tan.

Chapter 4

Syllabication: Prefixes, Suffixes, and Accent

Learning to read is a long term developmental process, and teaching the total word-analysis skills program is also developmental in nature. Previous chapters have presented data on letter-sound relationships. This chapter deals with skills which might be taught at various points on a continuum which represents word-analysis instruction. The skills deal primarily with syllabication; and accent, which involves noting structural changes in words, identifying pronounceable units within words, and noting degree of stress on these word parts.

SYLLABICATION

A syllable is a vowel or a group of letters containing a vowel sound which together form a pronounceable unit. The ability to break words into syllables is an important word-analysis skill which cuts across both phonic and structural analysis. Syllabication is an aid in:
1. pronouncing words not instantly recognized as sight words,
2. arriving at correct spelling of many words,
3. breaking words at the end of a line of writing.

Two major clues to syllabication are prefixes-suffixes, and certain vowel-consonant behavior in written words. Thus, the ability to solve the pronunciations represented by many longer printed words is built on the recognition of both structural and phonetic features of words. With practice, syllabication tends to become an automatic process. To illustrate, there will be considerable agreement among adult readers when they pronounce the following nonsense words: presemtur, obtenfab, besmorative, pammurly. (The syllabication patterns arrived at would probably be: pre·sem·tur; ob·ten·fab; bes·mo·ra·tive; pam·mur·ly). In addition, there would probably be relatively high agreement as to which syllable was to receive the primary accent: pre·sem'·tur; ob'·ten·fab; bes·mo'·ra·tive; pam·mur'·ly.

The reader's pronunciation of these nonsense words probably did not involve calling to mind rules which might be applied. Yet, the responses made were undoubtedly conditioned by previous learnings and experiences which relate to principles of syllabication. Despite the fact that there are numerous exceptions to some generalizations dealing with syllabication, others may be useful to pupils aspiring to become independent readers. A number of the more common generalizations covering syllabication will be cited and illustrated.

RULES FOR BREAKING WORDS INTO SYLLABLES

RULE I: There are as many syllables as there are vowel *sounds.* Syllables are determined by the vowel sounds heard—not by the number of vowels seen.

	No. of vowels seen	No. of vowels heard		No. of vowels seen	No. of vowels heard
phonics	(2)	fŏn ĭks 2	cheese	(3)	chēz 1
write	(2)	rīt 1	which	(1)	hwĭch 1
release	(4)	rē lēs 2	precaution	(5)	prē kô shŭn 3

RULE II: Syllables divide between double consonants—or between two consonants.

hap · pen	can · non	sud · den	ves · sel	vol · ley	com · mand
bas · ket	tar · get	cin · der	har · bor	tim · ber	wig · wam

List of words in which rule holds:

little	sudden	tunnel	after	window	candy
summer	cattle	button	pencil	canvas	basket
daddy	supper	robber	corner	silver	master
lesson	dollar	barrel	number	person	center
rabbit	bottom	valley	garden	napkin	silver
funny	letter	rubber	harbor	cargo	wander
carrot	ribbon	follow	picnic	chimney	circus
common	grammar	settle	submit	thunder	husband
suggest	copper	ladder	donkey	object	walrus

RULE III: A single consonant between vowels usually goes with the second vowel.

fa mous	ho tel	di rect	pu pil	ti ger	ce ment
ea ger	wa ter	po lice	spi der	lo cate	va cant

Common words which follow rule:

a round	pi rate	ra dar	be cause	a lone
be gin	fi nal	be fore	pi lot	li bel
pa rade	e lect	re ceive	lo cal	sta tion
mo ment	ba by	di rect	me ter	to day
fro zen	spi der	se vere	sto ry	so lo
ma rine	a bout	de cide	fa tal	si l ent

Note: Although this rule is cited extensively in the literature on reading, the exceptions to it are numerous.

RULE IV: As a general rule, do not divide consonant digraphs (*ch*, *th*, etc.) and consonant blends.

tea*ch* er	wea*th* er	ma *ch*ine	se *c*ret	a *gr*ee
bro*th* er	prea*ch* er	a*th* lete	coun *tr*y	cel e *br*ate

RULE V: The word endings, *-ble, -cle, -dle, -gle, -kle, -ple, -tle, -zle* constitute the final syllable.

mar ble	mus cle	han dle	sin gle	an kle	tem ple
ket tle	puz zle	no ble	pur ple	bat tle	bu gle

Following is a list of words which can be used in building board- or seat-work exercises. Instruct your students to practice on these words so that they can recognize and pronounce each one instantly. Point out how easy it is to learn to spell these words.

no ble	rat tle	sin gle	han dle	tem ple	an kle
mar ble	ket tle	wig gle	mid dle	ma ple	spar kle
sta ble	ti tle	jun gle	pad dle	ap ple	wrin kle
tum ble	bat tle	strug gle	bun dle	sam ple	sprin kle
trou ble	bot tle	gig gle	fid dle	pur ple	crin kle
fa ble	gen tle	bu gle	bri dle	stee ple	tin kle
dou ble	cat tle	ea gle	nee dle	sim ple	puz zle
rum ble	man tle	an gle	sad dle	un cle	fiz zle
peb ble	set tle	shin gle	kin dle	cir cle	muz zle
bub ble	lit tle	strag gle	pud dle	ve hi cle	daz zle

RULE VI: In general, prefixes and suffixes form separate syllables.

re load *ing*	*un* fair	*dis* agree *ment*	*pre* heat *ed*
hope *less*	*trans* port *able*	*un* like *ly*	ex cite *ment*

Note: Rules I and II above are often combined: Divide *between* two consonants and in *front* of one.

There are a number of suffixes which appear with high frequency in English words. Instant recognition of these word endings is a considerable help in word analysis. Fortunately, a number are extremely consistent in that they are always *pronounced* the same and always constitute the final syllable. The following list of words ending in -*ment*, -*tive*, -*tion*, -*sion*, -*ous* may be used in a number of ways to help children *see* and *hear* common phonic elements in words. These exercises can provide practice in:

1. sight-word recognition (read down the columns as rapidly as possible)

2. sounding longer words (those not instantly recognized as sight words)

3. breaking words into syllables

4. spelling of words (in conjunction with Items 2 and 3 above).

Word list for practice of sight recognition and pronunciation of words ending in -*ment* — always pronounced as in: move *ment*, a part *ment*:

payment	treatment	movement	measurement
statement	pavement	amusement	excitement
enrollment	monument	element	announcement
amazement	punishment	investment	refreshment
basement	equipment	department	agreement
improvement	resentment	management	government
argument	apartment	enjoyment	assignment
moment	advertisement	document	astonishment
settlement	adjustment	amendment	instrument

The word ending -*tion* — always pronounced *shun*:

lotion	motion	education	exception
invention	selection	mention	edition
election	promotion	condition	situation
location	friction	formation	section
direction	construction	subtraction	nation
attraction	vacation	foundation	solution
operation	fraction	position	objection
question	collection	intention	production
addition	population	affection	station

The word ending -*tive* — always pronounced -*tiv*:

active	locomotive	objective	relative
positive	destructive	elective	motive
native	adjective	sensitive	attractive
detective	legislative	protective	creative
talkative	attentive	executive	selective

The word ending *-ous* is generally unstressed *ŭs*:

dangerous	curious	enormous	courteous
previous	nervous	poisonous	prosperous
furious	generous	studious	numerous
mysterious	continuous	industrious	tedious

TEACHING PREFIXES AND SUFFIXES AS UNITS

The teaching of prefixes and suffixes involves dealing with a number of word-analysis skills which might be discussed under *structural analysis, phonic analysis,* or *syllabication.* Prefixes and suffixes are structural changes appended to root words. As such, they are also phonic units and, in a majority of cases, constitute syllables.

The first words children learn in reading are root words (look, come, run, talk), but even in grade one, they are systematically introduced to a number of inflectional endings: look*ed*, com*ing*, talk*s*, happ*ily*. As a child successfully progresses in reading, he will meet numerous prefixes and suffixes. Teaching these units must involve both structure and meaning. Generalizations about prefixes and suffixes are discussed below.

1. Common endings which begin with a vowel (-er, -est, -ing, -en, -able) are usually sounded as syllables.

2. One-vowel words ending in a single consonant usually double that consonant before adding an ending which begins with a vowel (run — running; stop — stopped; beg — beggar).

This fact may be taught as either structural or phonic analysis. Learning may be facilitated through board-work or seat-work exercises. The above rule may be illustrated as follows:

Table 11

Root	Add endings: -ed	-ing	Other endings: -ar, -er, -art, -ery, -ist, -ary, etc.
beg	begged	begging	beggar
dim	dimmed	dimming	dimmer
stop	stopped	stopping	stopper
slip	slipped	slipping	slippery
drug	drugged	drugging	druggist
can	canned	canning	cannery
sum	summed	summing	summary

Table 11 (Continued)

Root	Add endings: -ed	-ing	Other endings: -ar, -er, -art, -ery, -ist, -ary, etc.
trot			
brag			
plan			
rip			
log			
slim			

Other words which may be used in exercises:

ship, chop, trap, bat, spot, skin, stir, flap, fan, pit, cop, pad, rap, bag, snag, map, pat, hop, hug, fun, top, hot, tag, nap, pet, mop, bet.

Inflectional endings involve changes in visual patterns, meanings, and phonic elements. The objective in teaching these units is to have the child see the structural changes involved and associate the proper language sounds with the letter combinations. These sounds are already known by the child from his language experiences involved in speaking and listening. What is known must now be extended to the printed form of language.

3. Prefixes added to words give us new words — often with quite different meanings: clean, *un*clean; read, *re*read; place, *dis*place. Suffixes are word endings which, when added to root words, give us different words. Some of these cause radical changes in meaning (hope, hope-*less*); others simply give us words which perform different grammatical functions (happy, happily; luck, lucky, luckily).

The teaching of reading will of necessity have to focus on the changes in meaning which result when affixes are added to root words. Here we deal only with the changes in visual patterns as these relate to recognition and analysis. Many children develop the attitude that they will be unsuccessful in solving longer polysyllabic words and they give up easily. The reader can be given hints which will help him unlock such words and in turn bolster his confidence.

One way to achieve this goal is to lead the reader to see that English writing contains many prefabricated units which when added to words are always: (1) spelled the same, (2) are usually syllables, and (3) are pronounced the same. Successful readers tend to develop a visual awareness of prefixes and common word endings. After many experiences the process of instant recognition of units such as *pre, ex, con, ment, tion,* becomes fixed. Table 11 illustrates several approaches which might be used to emphasize recognition of such units.

Table 12-A

The first word in each column is a root word, the second has a common prefix, the third, a common word ending.

Root	*+ dis*	*+ ment*
appoint	dis/appoint	dis/appoint/ment
agree	dis/agree	dis/agree/ment
color	dis/color	dis/color/ment

Root	*+ re*	*+ able*
clean	re/clean	re/clean/able
use	re/use	re/use/able
charge	re/charge	re/charge/able

Root	*+ in*	*+ ness*
complete	in/complete	in/complete/ness
direct	in/direct	in/direct/ness
visible	in/visible	in/visible/ness
human	in/human	in/human/ness

Table 12-B

Note the italicized parts of the first word in each column. The words in a given column begin and end with the same prefix and suffix and in every case are pronounced exactly the same. Reading down the columns, pronounce these words as rapidly as you can. This practice should help you to recognize and "sound out" such words when you meet them in your reading.

con*duction*	*re*fill*able*	*dis*appoint*ment*
conformation	remarkable	disagreement
condensation	reclaimable	disarmament
conservation	recoverable	disarrangement
concentration	redeemable	displacement
conscription	recallable	disfigurement
contraction	respectable	discouragement
contribution	reliable	disenchantment
conviction	renewable	dislodgement
consolidation	restrainable	discontentment

Table 12-C

The following words contain prefixes and suffixes, but the words are in mixed order. Also, some prefixes-suffixes not found in *Part A* are introduced. Practice pronouncing the words as rapidly as you can.

dishonorable	resentment	discernment	remorseless
relentless	preoccupation	resistant	presumably
premeditate	consolidation	distractable	configuration
reconstruction	distributive	preparatory	reelection
protective	recollection	consignment	disqualification
confederation	presumably	prohibitive	constructive
unseasonable	imperfection	automotive	protectorate
implication	discoloration	concealment	unwholesome

FORMING PLURALS

1. Most plurals are formed by adding *s* to the root word: words, boys, trees, birds, cars, houses, periods, schools, paints, teachers, desks, books, girls, pets.

2. Add *es* to words which end in: *s, ss, ch, sh, x.*

s	*ss*	*ch*	*sh*	*x*
bus	dress	lunch	dish	fox
busses	dresses	lunches	dishes	foxes

3. When words end with *y* — change the *y* to *i* — then add *es.*

fly — flies; army — armies; penny — pennies

Examples of board- or seat-work exercises follow:

A. When words end in *s, ss, ch, sh, x,* plurals are formed by adding *es.* Write the plural for each of the following words. Note how the plural looks.

box	boxes	kiss	_____	wish	_____
glass	_____	couch	_____	class	_____
bench	_____	inch	_____	flash	_____
peach	_____	splash	_____	brush	_____

Other stimulus words appropriate for this exercise:

branch, pass, witch, fox, speech, brush, guess, loss, watch, ditch, wash, sketch, gas, ax, ranch, mess, tax, bunch, miss, mix

B. When a word ends in *y*, its plural is formed by changing the *y* to *i* and adding *es*. Write the plural for each of the following words:

fly _____	candy _____	body _____
baby _____	party _____	lady _____
puppy _____	cry _____	fairy _____

(cooky, kitty, family, funny, grocery, beauty, buddy, canary, city, dairy, cherry, jelly, factory, enemy, berry, copy, country, dolly, salary, daisy)

C. To form plurals of these words you may add *s*, *es*, or change final *y* to *i* then add *es*. Write the plural form for each word:

tax _____	city _____	dress _____
tree _____	match _____	skirt _____
pass _____	copy _____	dish _____

Adding Suffixes Following y or Final e

1. Change *y* to *i* before adding a suffix beginning with a vowel.

Word	*Common endings beginning with a vowel:*		
	-ed	-er	-est	-ous
busy:	busied	busier	busiest	
fury:				furious
dry:	dried	drier	driest	
muddy:	muddied	muddier	muddiest	
happy:		happier	happiest	
glory:				glorious
carry:	carried	carrier		

2. Exception: If the suffix begins with *i*, leave the *y*.

   crying, drying, frying, flying, copying, carrying

3. Drop final *e* before adding a suffix beginning with a vowel.

   large + er = larger; + est = largest.
   hate + ing = hating; + ed = hated.
   wide + er = wider; + est = widest.

COMPOUND WORDS

A large number of English words are formed by combining two words. While a relatively small number of compounds are encountered

in beginning reading, beyond this stage more and more of these words
are met. Recognition of compound words is achieved through every
type of word-analysis skill (structural analysis, phonic analysis, and
context examination). When teaching compound words, each of these
aids should be employed. It should be noted particularly that learning
sight words and structural-phonic analysis go hand in hand. The
following points should be kept in mind:

1. Compound words are part of the child's speaking and meaning
vocabulary. When he meets compounds in reading, he will combine
recognition and sounding techniques.

2. The meaning of compound words is derived from combining two
words.

3. The pronunciation of the compound word remains the same as
the two combining forms (except for accent or stress).

Procedures for teaching compound words will vary with the
instruction level. A few techniques are illustrated:

A	B
in	to
any	one
some	thing
door	way

1. Place words in Columns A and B on board.

2. "Here are some words we have learned as sight words — let's
read these words together."

3. "Sometimes we combine two words to make a new word — we
call these words compound words." (Combine words in A and B; ask
children to pronounce each word. Ask various children to use the
compound word in a sentence.)

in to — into	some thing — something
any one — anyone	door way — doorway

4. Seat-work exercises may be developed to parallel above.

A. "See the words under A and B — write them together to form
a new word."

A	B	C
up	on	upon
some	time	_____
him	self	_____
mail	box	_____

	A	B	C
	after	noon	_____
	hat	box	_____

B. "Each word in Column 1 can be placed with a word in Column 2 to make a new word (or compound word). The first one is done for you."

1	2	3
*rain	plane	*raincoat
sail	out	_____
air	*coat	_____
every	body	_____
with	boat	_____

C. "In your own words, write a definition for each of the compound words below."

1. beeswax: "_____."
2. rowboat: "_____."
3. drawbridge: "_____."
4. spellbound: "_____."
5. sharpshooter: "_____."

D. One of the words at the right will combine with all of the words in one column below. Write that word on the blank space to form a compound word.

bath
door
board
boat

_____way	sail_____	_____room	out_____
_____man	row_____	_____tub	over_____
_____step	steam_____	_____mat	score_____
_____stop	motor_____	_____house	chess_____

Compound words for board- or seat-work exercises:

Primary level			*Intermediate level*		
anyway	anyone	upset	salesman	downpour	blacksmith
something	evergreen	without	lifetime	fingertip	notebook
whenever	afternoon	birthday	lighthouse	shortstop	highpower
himself	airport	basketball	countryside	houseboat	blowout
snowman	sandbox	swordfish	peppermint	floodlight	taxpayer
windshield	herself	clubhouse	grasshopper	otherwise	overgrown
toothbrush	railroad	upstairs	flagpole	eyeball	riverbank
motorcycle	bookcase	barefoot	peacetime	pigtail	undersize
broadcast	horseshoe	typewriter	lifejacket	classmate	toothache
aircraft	lighthouse	anthill	northwest	slowpoke	marksman

FINDING LITTLE WORDS IN BIG WORDS

In the past, considerable confusion has arisen over this particular practice. It was once quite common, in materials prepared for teachers, to suggest that children be taught to "look for little words in big words." The theory was that after a child has learned to recognize smaller words, it would be useful to him as a reader if he would "see" these smaller units when they were part of larger words. This, it was alleged, would help him solve or pronounce the larger words.

This practice, of course, has only very limited utility or justification. It is justifiable when dealing with compound words or known root words to which have been added prefixes or suffixes. However, in general, the habit of seeing little words in big words will actually interfere with sounding out words in a great number of instances. This is true even in beginning reading; but once a child is beyond this stage, this practice has practically no justification whatsoever.

To illustrate, let us look at some of the more common "little words." In each of the following, if the child sees and pronounces the little word, he cannot arrive at the pronunciation of the word under attack.

at:	bo at	b at h	pl at e	o at	at e	at omic
	r at e	po ta to	co at	at hlete	he at	
as:	bo as t	ple as e	As ia	co as t	as hore	
on:	on e	t on e	d on e	h on ey	st on e	
he:	he at	he lp	c he st	bat he	t he y	w he at
me:	me at	a me n	ca me	sa me	a me nd	

Hundreds of other examples could be added using the above and other little words such as: *in, an, it, am, if, us, is, to, up, go, no, lid, are, or,* etc. Little words (or their spellings) occur frequently in larger polysyllabic words, but the pronounceable autonomy of the little words in big words is often lost. Therefore teaching children to "look for little words in big words" has little justification from the standpoint of phonic or structural analysis.

ACCENT

Each syllable in polysyllabic words is not spoken with the same force or stress. These variations in stress are called "accent." The syllable which receives the most stress is said to have the *primary* accent (car′ pen ter). Other syllables in a given word may have a secondary (lesser) accent, or syllables may be unaccented (in′ vi ta′ tion).

Teaching *accent* is usually reserved for the later stages of word analysis. The majority of words met in beginning reading consist of one or two syllables. Longer words met are those which a child has probably heard or spoken hundreds of times (yesterday, grandmother, afternoon, tomorrow, telephone).

Accent is important in using a dictionary when the objective is to determine the pronunciation of a word. It is important in reading when a child meets a word he does not know on sight but has heard and whose meaning he knows. For instance, if a child has heard or used the word "celebration" or "appendicitis," but does not recognize the printed symbols, he may distort its pronunciation through improper syllabication: cē le' bra tion, ce leb' ra tion; or improper accent: ap' pen *di'* ci tis.

Skills to be taught include:

1. How to read primary- and secondary-accent marks in the dictionary.

2. The habit of "trying" different soundings if the first attempt does not result in a known word.

3. The use of "clues" or rules of accent in attempting the pronunciation of words. Some of these follow:

a) In compound words, the primary accent usually falls on (or within) the first word (sail' boat; wolf' hound; fish' er man; door' way; police' man).

b) In two-syllable words containing a double consonant, the accent usually falls on the first syllable (cop' per; mil' lion; pret' ty; val' ley; sud' den).

c) When *ck* ends a syllable, that syllable is usually accented (chick' en; rock' et; pack' age; nick' el; mack' er el).

d) Syllables comprised of a consonant plus *le* are usually not accented (ble, cle, dle, gle, ple, tle). Many of the instances covered by the above rules might be summarized under one inclusive generalization:

In two-syllable root words, the accent usually falls on the first syllable —except when the second syllable contains two vowels.

(Exceptions occur in a number of words in which the last syllable contains two vowels — particularly if one is final *e*: be lieve'; pa rade'; sur prise'; sus tain'; ma chine'; sup pose'.)

e) Prefixes and suffixes, as a rule, are not accented (lone' ly; un hap' pi ly; re fresh' ment; dis re spect' ful; re tract' a ble).

f) Two-syllable words ending with *y* are usually accented on the first syllable (cit' y; ear' ly; ba' by; can' dy; sto' ry; par' ty; fun' ny; mer' ry; tru' ly).

Shift In Accent

A. Adding suffixes to some longer words may cause a shift in the primary accent. Words in column *A* have the primary accent on the first or second syllables, but in column *B* (derived forms) the accent has shifted.

A	B
u′ ni verse	u ni ver′ sal
mi′ cro scope	mi cro scop′ ic
vac′ ci nate	vac ci na′ tion
ac′ ci dent	ac ci den′ tal
con firm′	con fir ma′ tion

Generalization:

In many longer words the primary acent falls on the syllable before the suffix.

(Exception: In most cases the primary accent falls two syllables before suffix -*ate*: ag′ gra vate; dom′ i nate; ed′ u cate; hes′ i tate; med′ i tate; op′ er ate.)

B. Homographs—and accent shift: (homo = same; graph = to write: homograph = same writing).

Homographs are words with identical spellings, different meanings, and, in some cases, different pronunciations. The sentences below contain homographs. It will be noted that usage or context determines the pronunciation. (Changes may take place in accent or in both accent and syllabication.)

present = pre/sent′, pres′/ent; content = con/tent′, con′/tent

1. The mayor was *present* to *present the* awards.
2. The editor was not *content* with the *content* of the article.
3. Always be careful to *address* the letter to the correct *address*.

The following words may be used in teaching exercises when context is provided.

lead — lead	live — live	object — object
close — close	excuse — excuse	read — read
protest — protest	wind — wind	contract — contract
perfect — perfect	subject — subject	combine — combine
convict — convict	annex — annex	produce — produce
permit — permit	rebel — rebel	conduct — conduct

STRESS ON WORDS WITHIN SENTENCES

When working on *accent of syllables within words*, one might point out the parallel of *stress* on words within sentences. While this is not usually seen as a word-analysis skill, it is a most important factor in mastering the reading process. Concomitant teaching of accent and stress may help the child understand both concepts. Simple sentences might be placed on the board. Children should read the sentences, place added stress on each underlined word, and note the effect of the stress on the melody of the sentence.

> *This* is very bad news.
> This is very bad *news*.
> This is *very* bad news.
> This is very *bad* news.

USE OF THE DICTIONARY—AS A WORD ATTACK SKILL

As the child becomes an independent reader, he is likely to meet a number of words which

1. he does not know or use in his speaking vocabulary
2. cannot be easily solved by applying phonic generalizations.

Since the dictionary is a source for the pronunciation of words, certain dictionary skills are, in effect, word-analysis skills. Effective use of the dictionary involves learning the speech equivalents of visual symbols including primary- and secondary-accent marks; diacritical marks such as the macron (–) (make = māk); the breve (⌣) (ăt); the schwa (ə) (ten dər); etc.

Different dictionaries and glossaries found in textbooks may use a variety of symbols, or phonetic spellings, all of which will have to be mastered. For example:

> technique: tek nēk; tĕk nēk; tek neek
> temperament: tem′pər ə mənt; tĕm pēr á ment

(For a discussion of the schwa sound, see page 61.)

The *pronunciation key* of the dictionary or dictionaries used should be taught. The dictionary will be of little value in arriving at the correct pronunciation of words if these various symbols are not mastered.

CONCLUSION

Many of the skills dealt with in this chapter involve helping the child transfer auditory-speech knowledge to decoding print, or to spelling words as he writes. The discussion has included suggestions for teaching syllabication, affixes and accent. The emphasis has been on the structural changes which take place in printed words and on the way instant recognition of certain spelling units will aid the reader in solving the pronunciation of polysyllabic words. Effective use of such cues does not depend on memorization of rules. However, general-izations may help the learner to note certain spelling patterns that remain consistent in hundreds of different words. Soon the need for the generalization diminishes as responses to these letter-patterns become automatic.

Learning accent, both within words and in sentences, is an integral part of learning oral language usage. Instruction related to reading focuses on what the reader may do when he meets words which are not yet included in either his speaking or listening vocabulary. In such cases he must turn to an authority such as a teacher, a parent, or the dictionary. Effective use of the dictionary is an essential supplementary tool in wide independent reading.

Chapter 5

Alternative Approaches to Cracking the Code

As noted earlier, much of the criticism of American reading instruction voiced during the past fifteen to twenty years has focused on phonics instruction in beginning reading. Basal readers, which were the chief instructional media during this period, actually provided for teaching necessary phonic skills. However, many basals delayed phonics instruction and introduced only a minimum of letter-sound analysis in grade one. The total phonics program was spread throughout the primary gardes.

One possible explanation for the minimal presentation of letter-sound analysis in beginning reading was the overemphasis of mechanistic drill on letter sounds found in reading instruction of the previous era. Certain practices tended to produce undesirable reading behaviors; and others such as the A B C method confused the child in his efforts to crack the code.

During the nineteenth century, beginning reading instruction focused on rote learning of the A B C's. Children were drilled and taught to recite the letter names which made up unknown words met in reading. It was believed that letter-naming would provide the necessary phonetic clues for arriving at the spoken word which the printed symbols represented. In essence, this was a spelling approach since letter "names" often had little resemblance to speech sounds represented by letters (come = see oh em ee = kum).

Beginning shortly before 1900 and continuing for several decades, emphasis shifted from drill on letter names to drill on the "sounds of the various letters." Children drilled on isolated letter sounds which had little relation to the sounds the letters actually represented in words:

ba	ca	da	fa	ga	ha
be	ce	de	fe	ge	he
bi	ci	di	fi	gi	hi

Representative of these phonic approaches was Rebecca Pollard's (1899) synthetic method. This method reduced initial reading instruction to a series of mechanical procedures which dealt with letter patterns smaller than English words. (It was this type of activity which Bloomfield later attacked after it was no longer practiced in reading instruction.)

Single letters were sounded in isolation which did result in distortions. To pronounce consonant sounds in isolation did involve "blending a vague vowel sound" as Bloomfield charged (3) (p=puh, d=duh, etc.).

In addition to stress on single letter sounds there was considerable emphasis on identical word endings or "word families" such as -am; -ick; -at; -ip; -ill, etc. This practice was very closely related to the modern day emphasis on a "regular spellings" approach discussed later.

These types of instruction did not produce facile readers. Some changes were certainly called for, but the reform that was instigated went beyond the actual abuses. Any letter-sound analysis (phonics) in the early stages of instruction was frowned upon. No doubt in the minds of some individuals phonics per se became suspect. Basal readers reflected the change in attitude by delaying phonics instruction. This gave rise to the widespread belief that children were taught exclusively a "sight-word method".

In addition to the fact that most basal materials introduced letter-sound analysis rather slowly, many teachers taught phonics skills with less than optimum efficiency. Their pre-service training was partly at fault, since reading instruction in general and phonics instruction in particular were quite often slighted. (1) (7)

Meagre professional training in reading instruction (see Austin, 2) coupled with grade-level oriented instructional materials often militated against teachers being conversant with the entire phonics program. Instruction in a given grade tended to cover only those skills provided in the texts designed for that grade. Practically every classroom contained pupils whose instructional needs did not match the graded program. Thus, as pupils advanced through the grades, deficiencies in letter-sound analysis were likely to go uncorrected.

CRITICISM LEADS TO NEW MATERIALS

The facts presented above are a part of the background which provided substance for criticism of reading instruction in the 1950's and early 1960's. Phonics instruction was a bona fide issue, and concomitantly with the on-going criticism a great number of phonics instructional materials were published. Many of these materials were designed primarily to supplement other programs such as existing basals.

However, in addition to the supplementary phonics materials, several "new approaches" to teaching reading also appeared. The purpose of the following discussion is to briefly analyze a number of new approaches which seek to achieve a common goal — code cracking — by using widely different means. The methods discussed are:

A Linguistic Approach (regular spellings)
i.t.a. (Initial Teaching Alphabet)
Words In Color
Programmed Reading
Diacritical Marking System

While each of these approaches is radically different from the other, they all have a number of common elements:

A. Each is in essence an approach to beginning reading instruction.
B. Each has the same goal, that of *Cracking the Code* (i.e., teaching letter-sound relationships).
C. Each has its own specific set of materials, the use of which is essential to the method.

A number of the approaches to be discussed incorporate systematic teaching of phonics as an integral part of the program (i.t.a., Programmed Reading, *Words in Color*). The linguistic or regular spelling approach stresses minimal letter-phoneme contrasts while avoiding the systematic teaching of letter-sound relationships. The child *sees, spells,* and *pronounces* regularly spelled words: cat, bat, rat, sat. He sees and hears the same pattern in many different words. It is apparently hoped that the many repetitions will result in the child arriving at the relationship between letter-patterns and sound-patterns they represent.

LINGUISTIC (REGULAR SPELLING) APPROACH

Linguistics is the scientific study of human language, and linguists define language as speech. Linguists study and record the speech sounds peculiar to a given language; the order in which speech sounds do and do not occur in words; the order in which words can and cannot occur in sentences; and the changes which have taken place in languages. Thus, linguists chart the *patterns* found in a language in order to arrive at its structure. Similarities and differences in both sounds and syntax have been established for various languages. Linguistics is a broad term which covers many orientations to the study of oral language.

No branch of the science of linguistics has concerned itself with the problem of how children learn to read. Nevertheless, any linguist can address himself to this problem and in recent years some linguists have done so. Their emphasis has been primarily on developing materials and methodology for *beginning reading instruction*.

Individuals functioning within the framework of linguistic science maintain a vigorous scientific approach both in their research and in reporting data. Unfortunately, linguists have been less successful in applying scientific method as they worked on instructional materials. Those linguists who have been involved with this problem have advanced several hypotheses which relate to methodology.

Premises of Linguistic Materials

Proscribing of Pictures in Beginning Materials. A minor premise, which is reflected in most of the teaching materials thus far prepared by linguists, is that pictures should be omitted from beginning reading materials. The assumption is that children might use the pictures for solving some unrecognized words and in so doing they would neglect the actual solving of the printed word symbols. This assumption, whether true or not, cannot be said to rest on any linguistic authority since there is nothing even remotely related to this issue in the science of linguistics. Thus far, neither critics of, nor proponents of the use of pictures can point to empirical data for support of their position.

Vocabulary Control — (Regular Spelling Concept). Undoubtedly one of the major premises of linguists, who have thus far prepared reading instruction materials, is that *initial* instruction should be based exclusively on a unique vocabulary-control principle. This principle is that in early reading instruction the child should meet only those words which enjoy "regular spellings," a term used to designate words in which printed letters represent "the most characteristic sound" associated with each letter.

The word *cat* would meet this criterion; but the word *cent* would be *irregular* since the *c* represents not the characteristic *k* sound but the sound usually represented by *s*. The spelling *bird* is irregular because the *i* represents a sound usually represented by *u* (burd) as does the *o* in *come* (kum).

Unfortunately, a large number of the English words we use most frequently in building even the simplest of sentences have irregular spellings. Examples include: *a, the, was, once, of, any, could, love, too, their, do, said, one, who, some, only, gone, live, father, give, many, are, would, come, head, both, again, been, have, they, there, to, get, should,* etc. Normal English sentences are difficult to build when one decides to use only words which follow regular spelling patterns. For example, in Bloomfield's material, after 66 words have been taught (roughly equivalent to three pre-primers in a representative basal series) one finds only the most contrived sentences and absolutely no story line:

> Pat had ham.
> Nat had jam.
> Sam had a cap.
> Dan had a hat.
> Sam ran.
> Can Sam tag Pam?
> Can Pam tag Sam?[1]

After 200 words have been learned, the child reads these sentences:
> Let Dan bat. Did Al get wet? Van had a pet cat. Get up Tad! Let
> us in, Sis! Sis, let us in! Let Sid pet a pup. (3:87)

Meaning Waived in Beginning Instruction. Both Bloomfield and Fries, who have developed materials based on regular spellings, reject the thesis that beginning reading instruction should be concerned with meaning. The rejection of meaning is not so much a well-founded pedagogical principle as it is an expediency when one is limited to using only those words which qualify as regular spellings.

Clarence Barnhart, co-author of *Let's Read,* states in the introduction:
> Bloomfield's system of teaching reading is a linguistic system.
> Essentially, a linguistic system of teaching reading separates the
> problem of the study of word-form from the study of word
> meaning. (3:9)

Bloomfield writes:
> Aside from their silliness, the stories in the child's first reader are
> of little use because the child is too busy with the mechanics of
> reading to get anything of the content. . . . This does not mean that
> we must forego the use of sentences and connected stories, but it

---

[1] Leonard Bloomfield and Clarence Barnhart, *Let's Read: A Linguistic Approach,* (Detroit: Wayne State University Press, 1961), p. 65.

does mean that these are not essential to the first steps. We need not fear to use disconnected words and even senseless syllables; and above all we must not, for the sake of a story, upset the child's scarcely formed habits by presenting him with irregularities of spelling for which he is not prepared. (3:34)

Fries was in essential agreement when he wrote *Linguistics and Reading.*

Seeking an extraneous interest in a story as a story during the earliest steps of reading is more likely to *hinder* than to help the efforts put forth by the reader himself. (8:199)

In a later writing Fries took the position:

...as a matter of fact the *primary objective* of our materials built upon linguistic understanding *is the ability to read for meanings.* (9:245)

A bit of prose is then cited in which 58 per cent of the running words follow regular spellings:

Nat is a cat.
Nat is fat.
Nat is a fat cat.

A portion of Fries' rationale for meaning follows:

The first sentence specifies the meaning of the word *Nat* by identifying it with the well-known animal, *cat.* For us this identification is that *Nat* is the cat's name.

Nat is a cat.

The second sentence adds to the meaning by asserting that this particular cat, *Nat,* has a special physical feature to be described as *fat.*

Nat is fat.

The third sentence adds more to the meaning by bringing the description and the identification together in one summary sentence.

Nat is a fat cat.

The three sentences are tied together into a sequence by the repetition of the word *Nat.* (9:246)

This rationale is built on impeccable logic and the application of linguistic principles. Yet, one might be pardoned for feeling that this defense of *Nat the fat cat* represents a victory for meaning that is more apparent than real.

Opposition to Phonics Instruction

Proponents of the regular-spelling approach to reading instruction have voiced criticism of phonics instruction (teaching relationship of letter-sounds). Much of their opposition is based on two erroneous premises. The first of these is the misconception voiced by Bloomfield that the purpose of phonics instruction is to teach the child how to *pronounce* words by teaching him speech sounds. Bloomfield writes:

> The inventors of these (phonic) methods confuse writing with speech. They plan the work as though the child were being taught to speak .... If a child has not learned to utter the speech sounds of our language, the only sensible course is to postpone reading until he has learned to speak. As a matter of fact, nearly all six-year-old children have long ago learned to speak their native language; they have no need whatever of the drill which is given by phonic methods. (3:27)

This issue has been discussed in Chapter One where it was stated that the purpose of phonic instruction is to teach the child to associate printed letter-symbols with known speech sounds. He does not apply phonic analysis in order to learn *how* to pronounce words. His problem is that he does not know *what spoken word* is represented by a particular pattern of letters. Phonic analysis leads him to this discovery. Only in this sense is phonics related to pronouncing words.

The second misconception about phonics which one finds in the writing of Bloomfield and others is found in their belief as to how phonics is taught. Bloomfield states:

> The second error of the phonic methods is that of isolating the speech sounds. The authors of these methods tell us to show the child a letter, for instance *t*, and to make him react by uttering the *t*–sound; that is the English speech sound which occurs at the beginning of a word like *two* or *ten*. This sound to be uttered either all by itself or else with an obscure vowel sound after it. (3:28)

This description of phonics instruction was valid for an earlier era, but this practice had largely disappeared by the time Bloomfield inveighed against it. It is true that one cannot separately pronounce letter sounds, which taken together constitute the pronunciation of English words, and children are not asked to do so. They are taught that a particular letter represents the same speech sound in many different words and they are invited to think or subvocalize this sound when the letter occurs in a word they are attempting to solve.

This teaching is not at all inconsistent with linguistic science. For example, linguists agree that the letter *l* has a characteristic identifiable sound in each of the words *l*ake, *l*et, *l*ike, *l*ock, and *l*uck, regardless of which vowel sound follows the *l*. The initial phoneme in each of these words, and thousands of others, will be transcribed /l/.

In order to crack the code, the beginning reader must come to much the same conclusion as does the linguist. Yet there is agreement with Bloomfield that "this does not mean that we are going to try to teach phonetics to young children." (3:28) But the child who does not solve the relationship which exists between the letter *l* and the pronunciation of each of the words *lake, let, like, lock, luck,* will never become an independent reader of English. (It is implied, of course, that he will also make dozens of other letter-sound associations.) The learner must associate printed symbols with speech sounds regardless of whether he receives instruction in phonics or regular spellings. Phonics instruction focuses on this crucial problem in a straightforward manner; it *teaches* these relationships. Instruction deliberately leads the child to *see* letters and *distinguish* the speech sounds that these letters represent *in printed words*.

For example, in teaching the association of printed *b* and the speech sound it represents in words, the child:

a) looks at some familiar words which begin with the letter *b*.
b) listens for and hears the sound represented by *b* at the beginning of each of these words as the teacher pronounces them.
c) pronounces these words himself, paying special heed to the initial sound represented by the letter *b*.
d) observes that other printed words which begin with *b* start with the same sound as do *boy, ball, but, baby* (or any other word which begins with *b* which he may elect to think of as a model).

TEACHING BASED ON REGULAR SPELLINGS

In the regular spelling approach the child is first taught letter recognition and letter names (*aye, bee, see, dee, ee, eff*). Bloomfield suggests both capital and small letters, while Fries advocates teaching capital letters only in initial instruction. After learning the letters in isolation, they are combined into words. "The child need not even be told that the combinations are words; and he should certainly not be required to recognize or read words. *All he needs to do is read off the names of the successive letters, from left to right.*" (Emphasis added, 3:36)

Now the child is ready to begin working his way through a series of words which end with identical letter-phoneme patterns (*can, fan, man, tan,* etc.). Bloomfield suggests that teaching proceed as follows:

1. Print and point to the word CAN
2. The child is to read the letters "see aye en."
3. The teacher states "now we have spelled the word. Now we are going to *read* it. This word is can. Read it *can.*"
4. Present another word from the "an family" such as tan. (3:41)

The aim of this teaching is to have the child distinguish between various words with the initial letter-sound as the SOLE KEY. However, the child is never DIRECTLY TAUGHT the association between the initial letter and the sound it represents in words. There is no question but that the child must learn this relationship in order to become an independent reader. The regular spelling approach seems to over rely on the visual cue of the letter and reciting the letter *name*, which is not the sound the letter represents.

There are some data that strongly suggest that the initial letter in combinations has a stronger cue value than do other letters. Marchbanks and Levin reported that the initial letter is the most important cue in recognizing letter clusters. The final letter was the next most important cue, the middle being the least important. (17)

Based on extensive work with beginning readers, McKee states:

> Time and time again the author has found that in reading connected discourse first grade pupils can unlock strange words easily without knowing any of the letter sound associations represented by vowels in those words ... all they did was apply the skill they had acquired in using context and consonant sounds together to call to mind the familiar spoken words for which the strange printed forms stand. (16:104)

The following paragraph will permit the reader to test his own ability to read material when certain letter clues are omitted.

Th-s m-t-r--l -s pr-s-nt-d w-th -ll v-w-ls m-ss-ng. Th- q--st--n -s, c-n y-- r--d th-s p-ss-g-? Dr. Paul McKee st-t-s th-t ch-ldr-n j-st b-g-nn-ng t- r--d c-n s-lv- -nkn-wn w-rds w-th th- h-lp -f c-nt-xt cl--s -nd s--nd-ng th- f-rst l-tt-r -f th- -nkn-wn w-rd.

The merits of combining context clues and the initial letter sound, which is usually a consonant and thus highly regular, are discussed on pp. 7-8, 19-20.

OVERLEARNING CERTAIN VISUAL-SOUND PATTERNS

Early instruction deals exclusively with words which follow consonant-vowel-consonant patterns, and with a few two-letter vowel-consonant words. In all such words the vowel represents only its short sound. The regularity achieved through this vocabulary control is advanced as the chief virtue of this approach. The mere fact that these patterns are overlearned will leave some children vulnerable when the *same printed patterns* are met in which syllabication or vowel sounds are different.

For example, children learn the word *an* and also drill on C.V.C. words which end with *an* (can, ban, pan, etc.). Some children, when they meet words which contain this letter configuration, will follow the pronunciation pattern they have learned: an gel, an noy, an cient;

can al, can oe, can e; ban ana. Many other family words lose their pronounceable autonomy when they appear in larger words.

at:	at • e, at • omic, at • hlete;	fat:	fat • al;	rat:	rat • io
am:	am • en, am • use, am • ong, am • aze, am • end				
*la*d:	lad • le, lad • y, lad • en				
*ca*p:	cap • able;	map:	map • le;	tap:	tap • er
*ro*b:	rob • ust, rob • ot, rob • e;	sob:	sob • er		
*ro*d:	rod • eo, rod • ent;	sod:	sod • a, sod • ium		
*ho*t:	hot • el				
hum:	hum • id, hum • an, hum • or				

CODE CRACKING WITH A MISSING INGREDIENT

The Bloomfield program, as found in *Let's Read*, consists of teaching 5000 words of which only 38 per cent are presented as regular spellings.[2] The first 97 lessons in *Let's Read* introduce words which enjoy regular spellings, while the last 148 lessons present irregular words. The issue of the high number of irregular spellings is raised because Bloomfield's suggestion relative to teaching these irregular words seems totally unrealistic.

Bloomfield states, "There is a great difference between the work of Lessons 1-97 and almost all the child's later work in reading. . . . when it comes to teaching irregular and special words, each word will demand a separate effort and separate practice. (3:206) Here is the point where this system comes face to face with its inherent weakness. Once the regularly spelled words have been introduced, teaching the balance of English words "demands a separate effort and separate practice." While these are rather vague directions, it is clear that the proponents of the system do not talk in terms of *transfer*.

The system not having taught letter-sound relationships cannot suggest that what was taught in practice with regularly spelled words will transfer to words which contain both regular and irregular patterns. The child who has been taught *phonics* (letter-sound relationships) will find he can apply something of what he has learned to a majority of the irregular words. It is also true that he should and will learn some irregular words as sight words simply because he meets them many times in his reading-for-meaning. He will learn many regularly spelled words as sight words for the same reason.

---

[2] It should be pointed out that Bloomfield applies much stricter criteria than is necessary if one's goal is teaching reading.

It is to be expected that some children will make the necessary letter-sound associations just as some did when phonics instruction was at a minimum. However, the educational issue is that many children did not learn this essential skill without systematic instruction and the regular spelling approach carries the same risk. The question might be raised that there is nothing to prevent teachers from teaching the initial letter-sound relationships when the regular spelling materials are being used. While this method would appear to be desirable, the point is that such a practice represents a major departure from *suggested* precedure.

In summary, the foregoing discussion has attempted to focus on some of the methodological or educational issues which merit attention when considering the linguistic–regular spelling approach. Criticism has been leveled at some of the proscriptions found in that approach such as: exclusive use of regularly spelled words and withholding high frequency irregular words; sacrificing of meaning in order to maintain this practice; and not teaching letter-sound relationships.

It is hoped that the reader will not infer that there is no virtue in focusing the learners' attention on regular spelling patterns or family words. Phonics instruction includes this instructional practice when teaching involves *mental substitution* or *thinking the sound*. Teaching children to see and hear the difference in words which vary by only one letter or one phoneme is not only defensible, it is desirable. However, data are lacking which would establish that beginning reading should rely *exclusively* on teaching regular spellings and refrain from teaching letter-sound relationships.

INITIAL TEACHING ALPHABET (i.t.a.)

The fact that English spelling does not parallel the speech sounds heard when words are pronounced, plus the fact that a given sound may be represented by a number of letters, poses a problem in learning to read English. One suggested approach to this problem has been alphabet revision. In order to achieve a more uniform letter-seen sound-heard relationship, Sir James Pitman of England, devised an augmented alphabet to be used only as an Initial Teaching Medium (i.t.m.)[3]

The augmented alphabet devised by Pitman dispenses with the letters *q* and *x* while adding 20 printed characters. While this 44 character alphabet contains a number of irregularities in phoneme-

---

[3] The terms augmented in Roman alphabet, Initial Teaching Alphabet (i.t.a.) and Initial Teaching Medium (i.t.m.) are synonomous.

grapheme relationships, it does approximate a one-to-one relationship between letters seen and speech sounds heard.

i.t.a. Medium or Method

Obviously, the Initial Teaching Alphabet taken by itself is not a method of teaching reading. When i.t.a. was first introduced in the United States, its proponents stressed that it was exclusively a medium and not a method. Downing in an article, "Common Misconceptions About i.t.a.," writes at considerable length on the issue. He states:

> To summarize this major point — i.t.a. is not a method of reading instruction and in particular, it is *not* to be associated with the synthetic phonics approach. On the contrary, i.t.a. is a system of printing for beginners books which may be used with any method — eclectic, phonics, look-say, language-experience, individualized, film strip, programmed learning, or any other. (5:494)

The point of view that i.t.a. as a *medium* can be used equally effective with any *method* ignores reality. The i.t.a. represents a redesigning of an existing alphabet with the express purpose in mind of having printed letter symbols consistently represent one speech sound. There is no question but that the 44 character Initial Teaching Alphabet presents more of a problem in visual recognition than does the 26 character traditional alphabet. The potential virtue of the medium lies in the approximate one-to-one relationship between printed symbol and speech sound represented. Unless children learn this relationship and use it, there would be little point in advocating the revised alphabet.

Yet, the designers of i.t.a., in order to evade being identified with one or the other side in the "sight-word vs. phonics method" controversy, maintain that i.t.a. can be used with either approach. Assume a reading method existed which relied on teaching whole words. It would be most difficult to find any justification for using i.t.a. as a beginning medium for teaching whole words if one is to transfer to traditional print after a year of instruction. What could possibly transfer? How would a child know that *wunz* was the same word as *once*, or that *waukt* equalled *walked*?

Methodological Practices Involved in i.t.a.

One might grant that the Augmented Alphabet, per se, is only a medium, not a method. However, the mere choice of instructional materials printed in i.t.a. represents an important methodological decision. This decision, if based on logic, would then be followed by methodological considerations which grow out of the original choice. The i.t.a. involves more than just the use of a modified orthography. There are several salient instructional features which are an integral part of i.t.a. methodology thus far used in American schools. A discussion of these follows:

1. Contrary to Downing's disavowal of phonics, there is a strong emphasis on phonics or the relationship between printed letters and the speech sounds they represent. As stated above, this is most logical, considering the purpose of the medium or revised alphabet. In initial instruction children are not taught letter names, but they are systematically taught the sounds represented by letters.[4]

2. Instruction in i.t.a. stresses children's writing (using i.t.a. symbols) from the very beginning of the instructional program. In light of the fact that the child is to transfer from i.t.a. to traditional print early in the second year of instruction, the question is often raised, why should he learn and *reinforce* the augmented alphabet in his own writing?

The extensive writing found in i.t.a. programs also relates to the phonics emphasis discussed above. Writing involves the spelling of words and spelling stresses the phonic analysis of letter-sound relationships. Thus, the early writing emphasis actually reinforced the use of phonic analysis.

Raising the issue of extensive writing in first grade is not an implied criticism. Research data may prove that this practice is sound and desirable. On the other hand, the extensive writing done by beginning readers taught by i.t.a. introduces a variable which may have considerable impact on pupil achievement in reading. If later experimentation establishes that early writing has a salutary effect on reading achievement, the emphasis on early writing in i.t.a. methodology will prove to be a contaminating factor in studies which compare i.t.a. results with other methodologies which include very little writing.

3. In i.t.a. instruction children learn only the lower case letters. Capitals are indicated simply by making the letter larger. Thus the child does not have to deal with two different symbols for the same letter (A a, B b, C c, D d, E e, F f, G g, H h) in the initial stages of

---

[4] In a memo prepared for teachers who were to use i.t.a. in the Bethlehem, Pa., studies, one finds: "Although each symbol in the Initial Teaching Alphabet has a name, symbol names are not taught. It has been seen that the child often becomes confused in *analyzing or synthesizing* words when he has a choice between a symbol name and a symbol sound. *Therefore, only the sound which is to be associated with a given symbol is taught.*" (emphasis added) A.J. Mazurkiewicz, *How To Write the Initial Teaching Alphabet*, ITA Corporation, 1963, p. 1.

learning to read and write. In essence, what this practice does is to *delay* for a time the child's need to master both sets of symbols. That the child must deal with both upper and lower case letters when he transfers from i.t.a. to traditional print is one possible cause for the discrepancy between hoped for and actual ease in transferring. (Discussed later in chapter.)

4. In the promotional materials for i.t.a. it is claimed that there is a high degree of compatibility between i.t.a. and traditional spellings and that it will facilitate the child's transferring from i.t.a. to regular print. In addition to the differences in typography, another fact often overlooked is that i.t.a. materials frequently resort to phonetic respellings of irregularly spelled words. A number of these respellings have nothing to do with the modified alphabet as will be seen in the following examples.

enough - - - - enuf	anyone - - - - - enywun	said - - - - - - - sed
come - - - - - - cum	once - - - - - - - wuns	large - - - - - - laǰ
next - - - - - - nekst	lovely - - - - - - luvly	many - - - - - - meny
George - - - - Jorj	more - - - - - - mor	crossed - - - - crosst
have - - - - - - hav	some - - - - - - sum	one - - - - - - - wun
six - - - - - - - - siks	mother - - - - - muther	money - - - - - muny

Some of these respellings change the visual pattern of words quite drastically, which will not facilitate transfer to traditional print and spelling. While this practice might result in a fast start in beginning reading, it will have minimal effects on children cracking the main code. Since they must eventually deal with irregular words, this practice of *temporary* respelling represents an easier, more logical substitute code.

In addition to the phonetic respellings which do not involve any of the new i.t.a. characters, many spelling changes involve a reshuffling of vowels. The vowel changes and transpositions are made in order that the spelling will follow the "two-vowel generalization" (when two vowels come together, the first has its long sound and the second is silent). A few examples follow:

also - - - - - - - auls œ	night - - - - - - n ie t	find - - - - - - - f ie nd
their - - - - - - - th æ r	so - - - - - - - - - s œ	siezed - - - - - s ee zd
there - - - - - - th æ r	idea - - - - - - - ie d ee a	wife - - - - - - - w ie f
I - - - - - - - - - ie	most - - - - - - m œ st	walked - - - - - w au kt
knows - - - - - n œ s	came - - - - - - c æ m	ate - - - - - - - - æ t

In order to compare the effectiveness of i.t.a. (as a medium) with that of traditional print, the factors discussed above would have to be held constant in both treatments. Failure to control the variables of amount of phonics, amount of children's writing, and respelling of irregular words, have been contaminating factors in many studies.

Transfer from i.t.a. to Traditional Orthography

Concurrently with the introduction and use of i.t.a. in America, there were assurances from many quarters that *transfer* from i.t.a. to traditional print would not pose a problem. This optimism was allegedly grounded on reports from England. While Downing of England was actively promoting the experimental use of i.t.a. in America, his writing in 1963, on the issue of transfer contained a note of caution. He stated:

> If teachers *opinions* are supported by the results of the objective tests conducted last month (March 1963), we may feel encouraged in our *hopes* that all children will pass through the transfer stage with success, but *we must urge the greatest caution in drawing final conclusion or taking action on the basis of this preliminary trial* .... (4:25)

In 1965, Downing was a bit more optimistic. "First results from our British i.t.a. research project seem to show that transfer is remarkably easy in reading and surprisingly effective in spelling." (5:500) Downing's earlier caution was vindicated by the outcome of studies in England and America. In the December, 1967, issue of *Elementary English* Downing states, "Although teacher's subjective impressions of the transition stage have suggested that it is smooth and effortless, test results show that i.t.a. students from about mid-second year until about mid-third year do not read t.o. as well as they read i.t.a. a few weeks or even months previously.... More specifically, the British experiments show that children are not transferring from i.t.a. to t.o. in quite the way originally predicted." (6:849)

Mazurkiewicz, reporting for the school years 1963–64 (18) and 1964–65 (19), found only 26 per cent and 50 per cent respectively of i.t.a. taught pupils making the transfer at the end of grade one. Hayes and Nemeth (14) report 74 per cent of their i.t.a. group transferring to traditional orthography at the conclusion of grade one.

ITA and Reading Achievement

It would be enlightening to establish what per cent of adult Americans are now, or at one time were, fully convinced that use of i.t.a. materials results in superior reading achievement. Downing feels that the misconception that i.t.a. is a panacea has been caused by "the many articles in popular magazines and newspapers and also perhaps from the excessive enthusiasm of some 'salesmen' of i.t.a." (5:492) These have likely been influential.

Claims by the official spokesman for this medium have also had some impact, as illustrated by the opening sentence of a promotional brochure: "Many four- and five-year-olds in England are now reading from 150 to 250 little books in their first year at school." The brochure points out that for the first time five-year-olds have, and use, their own library cards! "They may have a bit of trouble in reaching the shelves, but not apparently in reading the books."[5]

As stated earlier, phonics emphasis methods result in higher first grade reading achievement than do programs which do not include systematic phonics emphasis. Reading achievement resulting from the use of i.t.a. has failed to establish this medium as significantly superior to traditionally printed materials *in which methodology also stresses systematic phonics instruction.*

Data reported by Mazurkiewicz, which covered the first year study at Bethlehem, Pennsylvania, showed no significant difference in reading achievement between total groups taught by i.t.a. and traditional basal instruction. Data consistent with the above analysis have been reported by Hahn (13), Tanyzer and Alpert (21), Hayes and Nemeth (14), and Fry (11).

WORDS IN COLOR

Words in Color is a beginning reading program developed by Caleb Gattengo.(12) The regular alphabet and traditional spelling of words are retained. However, thirty-nine different colors, each representing a different speech sound, are used in the initial presentation of letters and words. All teaching is done either from the blackboard or from a series of twenty-nine wall charts.

Any letter or combination of letters which represent a given speech sound are shown on the wall charts in the same color. For instance, the long sound of A is spelled or represented by *a, ay, eigh, ea, ey, aigh, ei, ai.* These and other letters which represent the long sound of A would be colored deep green on the wall charts (or on the blackboard if the teacher elected to print the following words in color): g*a*te, s*ay*, w*eigh*, gr*ea*t, th*ey*, str*aigh*t, th*ei*r, m*ai*l.

A lavender color is used to represent the sound of *f* in *f*ish as well as *lf* in ha*lf*, *gh* in cou*gh*, *ff* in pu*ff* and *ph* in *ph*otograph.

Initially, children are not taught letter names, but they receive intensive drill on letter-sound associations. The five short vowel sounds are introduced first and are sounded in isolation: $a=ah$; $e=eh$, etc.

---

[5] *The Story of i.t.a.,* i.t.a. Publications, Inc., 20 East 46th Street, New York 17, N.Y.

Drill includes printing several vowel letters on the board (a separate color for each). The teacher will then point to or tap each of the letters in the series such as $a-a-e-e-a$ to which the class responds "ah – ah – eh – eh – ah." Systematic drill then continues stressing the blending of vowel and consonant letter-sounds to arrive at: "ah + tuh = at."

No Reading Material in Colored Print

One can only imagine how difficult it would be to set even the simplest story in colored print using the *Words In Color* code. There are no sustained reading materials printed in this code. Thus the only colored printing that the child will see are the wall charts, eight of which contain letter combinations and twenty-one which contain whole words but no sentences. It is theoretically possible, but not likely, that the teacher will write sustained story or chart material on the board using the color code. Assume she wished to write *Washington's Birthday*, she would have to assemble sixteen pieces of chalk each of a different color making sure she used them in the proper sequence.

Since the child reads nothing in color and the large wall code charts are available only in the classroom, it would appear that the more he learned to rely upon the color cues the less likely it would be that he ever became an independent reader.

Research Data Lacking

In essence *Words in Color* simply presents the existing *letter configurations* in COLOR while drilling the child on the relationship between letters and speech sounds (phonics). At the time this is written there have been no studies which suggest that adding color to the *regular letter configuration* aids children in beginning reading.

To learn how to read the child must learn to distinguish letter forms from each other, and associate printed letters with speech sounds. Assume a child profited from color rather than from letter-configuration. In such a case he could not transfer anything of value to regular reading situations in which all materials are *printed black-on-white*.

In order to evaluate the efficacy of the *Words in Color* approach, one would have to ascertain what increment in learning was traceable to the use of the large number of colors. To do this, a comparison would have to be made between two comparable groups of children, one group using *Words In Color* and the other black-on-white printing, WHILE

KEEPING THE AMOUNT OF PHONICS INSTRUCTION CONSTANT IN BOTH APPROACHES.

It is very difficult to visualize the use of thirty-nine colors in the spelling of words that children will meet in beginning reading. It is quite likely that some children will develop problems in the discrimination of just noticeable differences in colors such as: cadmium green, yellow green (No. 15), yellow green (No. 47), dark green, olive green, light green, deep green, emerald green (No. 45), emerald green (No. 26), leaf green, gray green, yellow ochre, brown ochre.

PROGRAMMED READING

Programmed materials in book form have been developed for teaching a wide assortment of facts, processes, and subject matter. The rationale of programming will not be discussed here other than to mention one of the salient features of this approach. Practically all programmed materials consist of a large series of very small steps on the learning continuum. Each step confronts the learner with a stimulus statement, a problem to be solved, or a relationship to be grasped. He is then immediately tested to see if he has learned what was presented and is informed of his success or failure on the test item. His responses determine to some degree what his next task will be (i.e., go back and review, do more items of the same nature, or go on to the next step).

Probably the most widely known programmed materials in the area of reading are those developed by Sullivan Associates (distributed by McGraw-Hill Book Co.). These materials consist of a pre-reading program which serves as a foundation for moving into the actual programmed material. The basic materials consist of twenty-one conventional sized workbooks which are divided equally between grades one, two, and three. Other supplementary story type materials have also been developed.

Programmed reading has considerable emphasis on phonics or code cracking. Before the child can actually move into the programmed workbooks he must have made considerable progress in letter recognition and in associating printed letters with the speech sounds they represent. The degree to which programmed reading stresses and depends upon phonic analysis is illustrated by the skills a child must have acquired in the pre-reading stage such as knowing:

1. the capital and small letters; being able to name these, which of course implies the ability to differentiate between letter forms.

2. how to print both capital and small letters.

3. that groups of letters represent words, that words are read from left to right, and that letters represent speech sounds.

4. the speech sounds which are associated with the letters *a, f, m, n, p, t, th,* and *i.*

5. a number of words including *yes, no, an, man, I, ant, mat, a, pin, pan, tan, thin, fat.* This prepares him to read sentences such as *I am a man, I am a mat, I am an ant, I am a pin, I am a pan, I am fat, I am thin.*

DIACRITICAL MARKING SYSTEM

A number of instructional materials for learning to read have attempted to circumvent the irrational spellings of English by using diacritical markings. Various suggestions have been made that additional graphic signs be added to traditional printing to serve as signaling devices. Certain marks were to provide clues as to the sound represented by a given letter. During the 1890's, diacritical marks were used extensively in both beginning reading materials and spelling tests.[6]

Fry (10) recently devised and tested a Diacritical Marking System (DMS) which follows a number of basic rules such as:

a) regular consonant sounds and short vowel sounds are not marked.

b) long vowel sounds are indicated by a macron (gō meet).

c) silent letters are indicated by a slash mark (feed knight).

d) vowels representing the schwa sound are indicated by a dot (gallon, catcher, locust).

e) consonant digraphs are underlined (church, ship, what).

This system preserves traditional spellings, but adds the diacritical marking symbols as clues to pronunciation. A series of investigations by Fry compared reading achievement of children taught by means of regular text and the same text with diacritical markings added. No significant differences in reading achievement were found at the end of first, second, or third grades. (11)

Frank C. Laubach devised an English writing system which is used extensively in many parts of the world where English is not the native tongue of the learner (*Learn English the New Way,* 15). No new letter symbols are utilized but the approach relies heavily on respelling of words and the use of the single slant line to indicate a long vowel sound. The following sentences illustrate these ideas.

Let's De/cla/r Wor on Bad Spelling

It re/qui/rz from fi/v too seven yearz for our stu/dents to learn to read se/re/us buuks, be/cauz our spelling iz so/ difficult.

---

[6] For further discussion see Nila B. Smith, *American Reading Instruction* (Newark, Delaware: International Reading Association, 1965), pp. 127–37.

Mo/r than haff ov our wurdz ar misspelld. This is why/ Ingglish spelling iz ten ti/mz az difficult az eny uther spelling in thu world.

No wunder so/ meny boyz and girlz fail in sckool, and be/cum embitterd at so/si/ety. . . .[7]

CONCLUSION

A limited number of new approaches to teaching beginning reading have been discussed. Each has a common goal which is teaching the child to "crack the code" of written English. Judged by the traditional laws of learning some of these methods appear a bit awkward. However, each has the redeeming humanitarian virtue of attempting to *temporarily* protect the child from the vagaries of English spellings. For example, i.t.a. changes both the code and word spellings while the linguistic regular spelling approach shelters the child from words spelled irregularly or irrationally. Each of the code cracking methods is in essence a crutch which does not change the task involved in learning to read. The linguistic approach has the added liability that it does not systematically teach letter-sound relationships. Some children will, of course, make this essential association, but those who do not must be taught this skill before they can become independent readers.

The many alternative approaches available for cracking the code might be interpreted as evidence that mastering the English system of writing poses a formidable challenge. There is no question that English spelling reform is long overdue. The present practice of attempting to teach *all* American youth to read and spell English is the foremost example of conspicuous consumption of a nation's resources since the building of the pyramids. Unfortunately for many children, the belief is still widely held that our economy can still afford this cruel waste.

Without doubt, the most patriotic and educationally sound endeavor that reading teachers, and their teachers, could follow would be to set a date a few years in the future and decline henceforth to teach another child to read traditional English writing. The brief delay suggested would provide time for a federal commission to devise a sweeping and thorough spelling reform of English.

This suggestion is not likely to be followed since man is a thinking animal; and he is now busily thinking of numerous "new approaches" to teach archaic English. Furthermore, the federal government has indicated its willingness to raise the ante in support of education. It would be unbecoming of educators not to attempt hundreds of new

[7] Laubach Literacy Fund, Publication Office, Box 131, Syracuse 10, N.Y.

and devious approaches to the problem rather than advocating the one logical (and eventually inevitable) solution.

References

(1) Aaron, Ira E., "What Teachers and Prospective Teachers Know about Phonic Generalizations," *Journal of Education Research*, 53 (May, 1960) 323–30.

(2) Austin, Mary C., et al., *The Torch Lighters: Tomorrow's Teachers of Reading.* Cambridge: Harvard University Press, 1961.

(3) Bloomfield, Leonard and Clarence Barnhart, *Let's Read: A Linguistic Approach.* Detroit: Wayne State University Press, 1961.

(4) Downing, John A., *Experiments With Pitman's Initial Teaching Alphabet in British Schools.* New York: Initial Teaching Alphabet Publications, Inc., 1963, p. 25.

(5) —————————, "Common Misconceptions about i.t.a.," *Elementary English*, XXXXII (May, 1965) 492–501.

(6) —————————, "Can i.t.a. Be Improved," *Elementary English*, XLIV (December, 1967), 849–55.

(7) Durkin, Delores, "Fundamental Principles Underlying Phonics Instruction," *International Reading Association Proceedings*, 10, 1965, 427–30.

(8) Fries, Charles C., *Linguistics and Reading.* New York: Holt, Rinehart & Winston, Inc., 1963.

(9) —————————, Linguistics and Reading Problems at the Junior High School Level," *Reading and Inquiry*, International Reading Association Proceedings, 10, 1965, 244–47.

(10) Fry, Edward, "A Diacritical Marking System To Aid Beginning Reading Instruction," *Elementary English*, XXXI (May, 1964) 526–29.

(11) —————————, *Comparison of Three Methods of Reading Instruction* (ITA, DMS, T.O.), USOE Cooperative Research Project, No. 3050, 1967.

(12) Gattengo, Caleb, *Words In Color*. Chicago: Learning Materials, Inc., 1962.

(13) Hahn, Harry T., *A Study of the Relative Effectiveness of Three Methods of Teaching Reading In Grade One*, USOE Cooperative Research Project, No. 2687, 1965.

(14) Hayes, Robert B. and Joseph S. Nemeth, *An Attempt to Secure Additional Evidence Concerning Factors Affecting Learning to Read*, USOE Cooperative Research Project, No. 2697, 1965, 34.

(15) Laubach, Frank C., *Learn English the New Way*, (Book I, II). Syracuse 10, N. Y.: New Readers Press, Box 131.

(16) McKee, Paul and William K. Durr, *Reading: A Program of Instruction for the Elementary School*. Boston: Houghton Mifflin Company, 1966.

(17) Marchbanks, Gabrielle and Harry Levin, "Cues by Which Children Recognize Words," *Journal of Educational Psychology*, 56 (April, 1965) 57–67.

(18) Mazurkiewicz, Albert J., "Lehigh-Bethlehem — I/T/A Study Interim Report Six," *Journal of the Reading Specialist*, 4 (September 1964), 3–6.

(19) _____, *First Grade Reading Using Modified Co-Basal Versus the Initial Teaching Alphabet*, USOE Cooperative Research Project, No. 2676, 1965.

(20) Smith, Nila Banton, *American Reading Instruction*. Newark, Delaware: International Reading Association, 1965, 127–37.

(21) Tanyzer, Harold J. and Harvey Alpert, *Effectiveness of Three Different Basal Reading Systems on First Grade Reading Achievement*, USOE Cooperative Research Project, No. 2720, 1965.

Bibliography

(A limited number of sources which contain suggestions for teaching phonics.)

Agnew, Donald C., *Effect of Varied Amounts of Phonetic Training on Primary Reading.* Durham, N.C.: Duke University Press, 1939.

Bagford, Jack, *Phonics: Its Role in Teaching Reading.* Iowa City: Sernoll, Inc., 1967.

Bear, David E., "Two Methods of Teaching Phonics: A Longitudinal Study," *Elementary School Journal,* 64 (February, 1964), 273-79.

Botel, Morton, "Strategies for Teaching Sound-Letter Relationships," *Vistas In Reading,* International Reading Association Proceedings 2, Part I, 1966, 156-59.

Brzeinski, Joseph E., "When Should Phonics Instruction Begin?", *Reading as an Intellectual Activity,* International Reading Association Proceedings, 8, 1963, 229-32.

Burrows, Alvina and Zyra Lourie, "When Two Vowels Go Walking," *Reading Teacher,* 17 (November, 1963) 79-82.

Chall, Jeanne, *Learning to Read: The Great Debate.* New York: McGraw-Hill Book Company, 1967.

Clymer, Theodore, "The Utility of Phonetic Generalizations in the Primary Grades," *Reading Teacher,* 16 (January, 1963) 252-58.

Cordts, Anna D., *Phonics for the Reading Teacher.* New York: Holt, Rinehart & Winston, Inc., 1965.

Cutts, Warren G., *Modern Reading Instruction.* Washington, D.C., The Center for Applied Research In Education, Inc., Chapters 3, 4.

Dechant, Emerald V., *Improving the Teaching of Reading.* Englewood Cliffs, N.J.: Prentice-Hall, Inc., 1964 (Chapters 10–11).

Durkin, Dolores, *Phonics and the Teaching of Reading,* Bureau of Publications, Teachers College, Columbia University, 1962.

Durrell, Donald D. (ed.), "First Grade Reading Success Study: A Summary," *Journal of Education,* 140: 3 (February, 1958).

First Grade Reading Programs, Perspectives In Reading No. 5, Newark, Delaware: International Reading Association, 1965.

Fry, Edward, "A Frequency Approach to Phonics," *Elementary English*, XXXXI (November, 1964) 759–65.

Gans, Roma, *Fact and Fiction About Phonics*. Indianapolis: The Bobbs-Merrill Co., Inc., 1964.

Glass, Gerald G., "The Teaching of Word Analysis Through Perceptual Conditioning," *Reading and Inquiry*, International Reading Association Proceedings, 10, 1965, 410–13.

Gray, William S., *On Their Own In Reading* (rev. ed.), Chicago: Scott, Foresman & Company, 1960.

Heilman, Arthur W., *Principles and Practices of Teaching Reading*, Second Edition, Columbus, Ohio: Charles E. Merrill Publishing Company, 1967 (Chapter 9).

Herr, Selma E., *Phonics Handbook for Teachers*. Los Angeles: E.R.A. Publishers, Inc., 1961.

Herrick, Virgil E. and Marcella Nerbovig, *Using Experience Charts with Children*. Columbus, Ohio: Charles E. Merrill Publishing Co., 1964.

Lamb, Pose, *Linguistics In Proper Perspective*. Columbus, Ohio: Charles E. Merrill Publishing Co., 1967.

May, Frank B., *Teaching Language as Communication to Children*. Columbus, Ohio: Charles E. Merrill Publishing Co., 1967.

McKee, Paul and William K. Durr, *Reading: A Program of Instruction for the Elementary School*. Boston: Houghton Mifflin Company, 1966.

Oaks, Ruth E., "A Study of the Vowel Situations In a Primary Vocabulary," *Education*, LXXII (May, 1952) 604–17.

Piekarz, Josephine A., "Common Sense about Phonics," *Reading Teacher*, 18 (November, 1964) 114–17.

Scott, Louise Binder and J.J. Thompson, *Phonics*. Manchester, Mo.: Webster Publishing, 1962.

Soffietti, James P., "Why Children Fail to Read: A Linguistic Analysis," *Harvard Educational Review*, 25 (Spring, 1955) 63–84.

Spache, George D., *Reading in the Elementary School*. Boston: Allyn and Bacon, Inc., 1964 (Chapter 12).

Stone, Clarence R., "Questionable Trends in Beginning Reading," *Elementary School Journal*, (January, 1966), 214–22.

Tinker, Miles A. and Constance M. McCullough, *Teaching Elementary Reading*. New York: Appleton-Century-Crofts, 1962 (Chapters 7, 20).

Wilson, Robert M. and MaryAnne Hall, *Programmed Word Attack For Teachers*. Columbus, Ohio: Charles E. Merrill Publishing Co., 1968.

Index

Aaron, Ira E., 114
Accent, 88-91
  rules governing, 89
  shift in, 90
Affixes, 81-84
Alpert, Harvey, 108-115
Alphabetic principle, 3
Auditory discrimination, 26-29
  previous experiences related to, 26
  teaching techniques, 27-29
  word list for teaching, 49-52
Austin, Mary C., 94, 114

Barnhart, Clarence, 66, 97, 114
Bailey, Mildred Hart, 25
Beginning reading:
  concomitant learnings, 11-12
  newer approaches, 95-112
Blends, 36-39
  final letters in words, 41, 42
Bloomfield, Leonard, 66, 94, 97, 99, 100, 102, 114
Burmeister, Lou E., 25
Burrows, Alvina T., 25

Chall, Jeanne, 9, 10, 11, 25
Clymer, Theodore, 25, 62
Code cracking:
  alternate approaches to, 93-112
  defined, 4
  linguistic approach, 95-103
Combining word analysis skills, 6-8

Compound words, 85-87
Consonant sounds, 31-52
  blends, initial, 36-39
  digraphs *(sh, wh, th, ch)*, 34-36 42
  final consonant sounds, 40-41
  final letters in words, 40-42
  generalizations covering, 47-48
  initial consonants, teaching of, 32-34
  irregular consonant sounds, 43-46
  prior to vowel sounds, rationale for, 31
  silent consonants, 44-46
  substitution of initial sounds, 39-40
  word list for teaching, 49-52
Context clues, 5-6, 7-8, 19, 20
Contractions, 46-47

Dale, Edgar, 18
Diacritical marking systems, 111-112
Dictionary, use of, 91
Differentiation of instruction, 21
Digraphs, 34-36, 42
Diphthongs, 70-71
Dolch Sight Word List, 18
Downing, John A., 104, 107, 114
Durkin, Delores, 66, 114
Durr, William K., 115

Educational issues, phonics, 8-21

code cracking "first," 9-11
differentiation of instruction, 21
overreliance on one skill not
    efficient, 12-15
principles for teaching, 21-23
rules, efficacy of, 15-16
sequence of teaching, 18-21
Emans, Robert, 25

Final e rule, 63-64
Fries, Charles C., 97, 98, 100
Fry, Edward, 108, 111, 114

Gattengo, Caleb, 108, 115
Grapheme-phoneme relationship, 3
Gray, William S., 20, 39

Hahn, Harry T., 107, 108, 115
Hayes, Robert B., 108, 115
Homonyms, 72

Initial Teaching Alphabet, 103-108
    medium or method, 104
    methodology in, 104-107
    reading achievement with, 107-108
    transfer, problem of, 107
Irregular letter-sound relationships:
    consonant digraphs, 34-36, 42
    consonants, 43-46
    discussion of, 13-15
    silent consonants, 44-46
    vowels, 13-15, 67-69

Lauback, Frank C., 111
Letter sounds:
    consonants, 31-51
    silent consonants, 44-46
    variability of, 13-15, 67-69, 72
    vowel sounds, 54-71
Levin, Harry, 101, 115
Linguistic approach:
    phonics instruction, opposition to,
        98-100
    premises of, 96-100
    teaching based on, 100-101
Little words in big words, 88

Lourie, Zyra, 25

McKee, Paul, 20, 101, 115
Marchbanks, Gabrielle, 101, 115
Mazurkiewicz, Albert J., 107, 108,
    115
Morphemes, defined, 4

Nemeth, Joseph S., 107, 108, 115

Oaks, Ruth E., 25
Overreliance on one skill, not
    efficient, 12-15

Phoneme, defined, 3
Phonetics, defined, 2
Phonic generalizations:
    accent, 88-90
    consonants, related to, 47-48
    vowels, 72-73
Phonics:
    differentiation of instruction, 21
    educational issues, 8-16
    overreliance not efficient, 12-15
    principles for teaching, 21-23
    purpose of, 1
    sequence for teaching, 18-21
    steps in teaching, 23-24
    test of skills, 75-76
Picture clues, 6
Pitman, Sir James, 103
Plurals, 84-85
Prefixes, 81-84
Programmed reading, 110-111
Principles for teaching phonics,
    21-23

Regular spelling approach, see
    Linguistic approach
Rhyming sounds, 28-29
Rules, phonics teaching:
    adjacent vowels, 61-63
    ay as final letters, 65
    final e rule, 63-64
    issues involved, 15-16
    utility of, 62

Schwa sound, 61
Sequence, teaching phonic skills, 18-21
Sight words, list of, 74
Sight word method, 2-3
Silent consonants, 44-46
Smith, Nila B., 111
Structural analysis:
  affixes as units, 81-84
  compound words, 85-87
  plurals, 84-85
  syllabication, 77-87
  word analysis, part of, 5
Syllabication, 77-87
  affixes as syllables, 81-84
  rules for, 78-79
  word lists for teaching, 80, 83-84

Tanyzer, Harold J., 108, 115

Utility of vowel rules, 62

Variability of letter sounds:
  consonant irregularities, 43-46
  homonyms, 72
  origins of, 13
  vowels, 13-14, 61-62, 67-69
Visual discrimination, 30-31
Vowel sounds, 53-75
  adjacent vowels, 61-63
  ay combination, 65
  diphthongs, 70-71
  exceptions to rules, 13-15, 62, 67-68
  exercise for teaching, 67

final *e* generalization, 63-65
initial and medial taught together, 60-61
long vowel sounds, 61-65
oo sounds, teaching of, 69
prior learnings, basis for teaching, 54
r controller, 68-69
schwa sound, 61
short sounds first, rationale for, 53
short sounds, medial position, 54-60
y functioning as a vowel, 65-66

Word analysis skills:
  definition of, 2
  discussion of, 4-8
  compound words, 85-87
  context clues, 5-6, 19
  dictionary, use of, 91
  picture clues, 6
  plurals, forming of, 84-85
  skills in combination, 6-8
  structural analysis, 5
  word form, 4-5
Word families, 57
Words In Color, 108-109
Word lists:
  consonant sounds, teaching of, 49-52
  sight words, 74
  syllabication, teaching, 78-81, 83-84
Whole words, rationale for teaching, 16-18